Made & Sold

LAURENCE KING

Published in 2009 by
Laurence King Publishing Ltd
361–373 City Road
London EC1V 1LR
United Kingdom
email: enquiries@laurenceking.com
www.laurenceking.com

A catalogue record for this book
is available from the British Library.

ISBN-13: 978 1 85669 628 9

Words and image selection:
Agathe Jacquillat and
Tomi Vollauschek at FL@33

Front cover image:
'Stitches' by Anne Brassier at Airside

Senior editor: Susie May

Book design: FL@33
www.flat33.com

Printed in China

Made & Sold

Toys, T-shirts, Prints, Zines and Other Stuff

Agathe Jacquillat and Tomi Vollauschek at FL@33

Laurence King Publishing

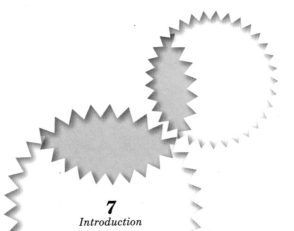

7

Introduction |

This book showcases an exciting selection of self-initiated sideline projects created by a new generation of multi-disciplinary practitioners who also work for commission or client-based projects. These young independent design studios, freelancers and commercial artists often state that the creation of self-initiated products informs their commissioned work and vice versa – and some do not make any distinction at all between these activities and consider both aspects of their work as an integral part of their creative process. Many of the talents showcased are, in many respects, their own clients and design, produce, manufacture and directly sell their very own sidelines – often online – to a potentially global customer base. This is not only a commercial, entrepreneurial or self-promotional activity but also satisfies their artistic needs for diversity and experimentation – often explained simply by designers and artists as a great way to stay sane, fresh and creative.

We interviewed the contributors and all – both emerging and established – unanimously stated that their main motivation to invest time and money into their sideline products was down to passion, the artistic urge and the resulting gratification gained from going the extra mile. Most stressed their desire for authorship and the potential opportunity for expressing their standpoints and making a mark. Pull-out quotes from the conducted interviews are featured throughout the book and give an intriguing insight into the underlying motivations and philosophies, as well as explaining how sideline activities fit into the daily business of running a design studio, work as freelancer or having a day job as an employee. We tried to feature at least one quote from each selected contributor and did, with a few exceptions, manage to incorporate at least one each.

One of the final questions was whether the contributors had any suggestions for an even better book title in addition to, or to replace, our chosen one. While almost everybody seemed to be happy with our choice, some made a few recommendations and we would like to share a few insightful favourites with you: 'Things We Do While You Are Asleep', 'Products by Graphic Designers, Illustrators and Artists', 'Sidekicks', 'Fertile Playground', 'We Won't Change The World But Make It Look Less Ugly', 'Alter Ego', 'Off The Page', 'After 5.30', 'Passion Fruits', 'Creative Obsessions' and last but not least 'Don't Give Up The Day Job'.

The book's chapters have been defined in a similar way to the sections within an online shop – thus projects are grouped according to this book's seven chapters: 'Books, Magazines and Zines', 'Toys', 'Posters, Prints and Canvases', 'Fonts and Typographic 3D Products', 'Clothing', 'Accessories' and 'Miscellaneous'.

While some of the products featured here were only produced in very small editions, others might even still be available – so please don't hesitate to visit the websites listed with each project.

We hope you find this selection of works by these passionate individuals, collectives and studios as inspiring as we do.

Agathe Jacquillat and Tomi Vollauschek, FL@33

Books, Magazines and Zines |

This chapter features a selection of extraordinary self-initiated publications from around the world, from artists' books, magazines and photocopied low-budget zines to glossy print releases – even a flipbook, a colouring-in book and collaborative projects – in both limited editions and larger print-runs. What they all have in common is that they have been lovingly edited and put together, often in the artists' spare time and at their own expense.

*'I would love to keep adding new products to my sideline projects in the future.
I'd love to create the same level of surprise in different media.'*
Masashi Kawamura

Masashi Kawamura |

masa-ka.com

Masashi Kawamura was born in Tokyo and raised in
San Francisco. After working for a time in Amsterdam,
he is now based in New York. *Rainbow In Your Hand*
started as a personal project in summer 2007, and was
soon published by Utrecht – a Japanese bookstore. It's
a flipbook, but instead of presenting an animation, it
allows you to create a three-dimensional rainbow. It was
featured on major websites and blogs such as Yahoo!
News, Cool Hunting and FFFFOUND!, and also on
Japanese television and in newspapers. The book won
an NY ADC Silver Cube in 2008.

| 72 pages, 130 x 60 mm (5⅛ x 2⅜ in)

I 10 pages, 197 x 270 mm (7¾ x 10⅝ in)

10 pages, 135 x 130 mm (5⅜ x 5⅛ in) I

'The work I do solely for myself definitely informs my commissioned work.'
Andy Smith

Andy Smith |
asmithillustration.com

Royal College of Art graduate Andy Smith combines illustration and typography to create images that have humour, energy and optimism. His time is split between commercial work and self-initiated projects such as silkscreen-printed posters and books. Featured here are some of the books that he hand screen-printed and bound. They are printed on textured recycled paper in matt and gloss inks which gives them a tactile, handmade quality.

Opposite page, top: *Fattys Big Bubble*, 2005, edition of 200

Opposite page, bottom: *We are the target people*, 2005, edition of 300 and *The Hi Tide*, 2008, edition of 100

Below: *Lightning Strikes at Fattys House*, 2006, edition of 300

I 12 pages, 135 x 130 mm (5⅜ x 5⅛ in)

10 pages, 135 x 130 mm (5⅜ x 5⅛ in) I

 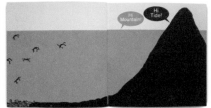  

HudsonBec | If You Could
hudsonbec.com
ifyoucould.co.uk

HudsonBec is an independent design studio set up by designers Will Hudson and Alex Bec. They are both 2007 graduates from Brighton University's graphic design course in the UK and have worked on their *If You Could* project since 2006.

Left: The first edition was a boxed collection of A5-sized cards. Launched in 2006, issue one features 21 internationally renowned illustrators, responding to the question 'If you could do anything tomorrow, what would it be?'. Printed in two-colour on 350 gsm stock, housed in a hand-editioned, shrink-wrapped clam-box.

Opposite page, top: The second edition was released in book form in 2007. Following an open call for entries, 112 artists' responses were selected for inclusion in this hand-editioned, full-colour, 160-page, perfect-bound publication.

Both editions, each of 1,000, are sold out.

| Edition one, Anthony Burrill

| Edition two, Ian Wright

'We like to have variety — as soon as you only do one thing there's a chance it'll become a chore, and we'd never like to find ourselves in that position.'
Will Hudson and Alex Bec, HudsonBec

Edition two, Geneviève Gauckler

Edition two, Supermundane

Edition two, Oliver Jeffers

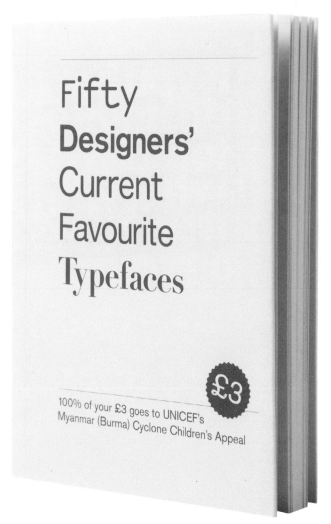

Fifty Designers' Current Favourite Typefaces

£3

100% of your £3 goes to UNICEF's Myanmar (Burma) Cyclone Children's Appeal

James West, Create/Reject |
createreject.com

Create/Reject was set up in 2006 by James West after he graduated from the London College of Communication. Most of his work is concept-driven for art, fashion and culture clients, and is continually supported by a stream of self-initiated work. Recent projects include *Fifty Designers' Current Favourite Typefaces* – a book featuring among others, Daniel Eatock, eBoy, Michael C. Place, Stefan Sagmeister and Wim Crouwel. West expected to sell about 50 copies online but instead all 2,000 sold out in the first two weeks, raising £6,000 for UNICEF.

'Designers are naturally intrigued by the world and the ways of interacting with it, and so it's an obvious action to explore lots of avenues of visual expression – some that require a client's brief, and some that require your own.'
James West, Create/Reject

Peepshow | Peepshop

peepshow.org.uk
peepshop.org.uk

Much of the collective's creative input for their commercial output stems from the extracurricular activities they engage in through various self-initiated exhibitions and events worldwide.

The product range by London-based Peepshow includes *Colour Me In Book* from 2008 – a 20-page colouring book by Miles Donovan featuring Blondie, Gary Numan, Hall and Oates, LL Cool J and many more. Limited edition of 50.

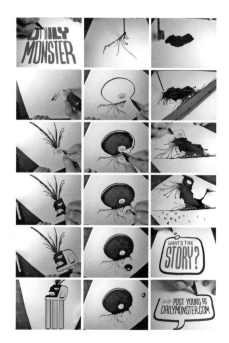

Stefan G. Bucher, 344 | Daily Monster
344design.com
dailymonster.com

Stefan G. Bucher, originally from Germany, is based in California where he runs his design studio 344. He is an award-winning designer and author, a brilliant monster illustrator and the Art Directors Club of New York even declared him a Young Gun in 2004. Bucher is the creator of the incredibly popular Daily Monster project.

DailyMonster.com started as a way to promote his *Upstairs Neighbors* book to publishers. In this it failed entirely. But the site became a much, much bigger thing in and of itself when people fell in love with the characters and started contributing stories. The biggest commercial product that has come out of the Daily Monster project has been the book, *100 Days of Monsters*, published in 2008 by HOW Books (224 pages with DVD, hardcover).

Cousins of the Monsters will also appear as a recurring segment of short drawing films on the Sesame Street Workshop's relaunch of the classic children's TV show *The Electric Company*.

'I've always wanted my own products, so I could control every aspect of the project from idea to illustration, writing and design. He who signs the cheques controls the type size.'
Stefan G. Bucher, 344 Design

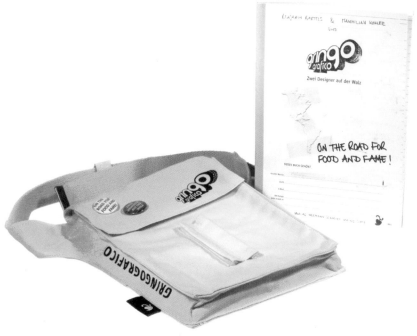

Benjamin Bartels and Max Kohler | Gringografico

gringografico.com
das-rheingold.de
benjamin-bartels.com

Benjamin Bartels and Max Kohler studied together in Wiesbaden, Germany, where they graduated in 2006. Their travel journal *Gringografico – on the road for food and fame!* is a road book about work and wanderlust that was published in 2007 by Hermann Schmidt Verlag.

In the twelfth century, German journeymen of various guilds would embark on a journey at the end of their apprenticeship (the *Walz*), to practice what they had learnt, to enhance their knowledge and to learn new things. Only those who did the *Walz* were allowed to become master craftsmen. Bartels and Kohler tried to apply this historic idea to their own modern craft. For six months and one day they travelled along the Pan-American Highway from Canada to Peru, stopping at various ad agencies and design studios looking for work. In exchange they would ask for a bite to eat and a place to sleep.

The award-winning *Gringografico* documents over 10,000 miles of highway travel with snapshots of the everyday life of two designers who firmly believe that instead of just waiting for something inspiring to happen they should instead go out there to find inspiration themselves.

BOOK SMARTS #1

THE TRUTH
ABOUT NOTHING

IT WON'T ALWAYS
GROW BACK.

SILENCE IS A
POWERFUL
STATEMENT.

SLEEP IS A NEAR
DEATH
EXPERIENCE.

BOOK SMARTS #2

SEMI-SURVIVAL
GUIDE TO THE
FUTURE

ASTRONOMERS
WILL NEED MORE
SPACE.

RADIO WILL WEAR
OUT ANOTHER
PERFECTLY GOOD
SONG.

A SCIENTIST
WILL BE CLONED.

BOOK SMARTS #3

WORDS OF
FINITE WISDOM

YOU BEAT
MILLIONS OF
SPERM TO GET
WHERE YOU ARE
TODAY.

ACT LIKE IT.

SOME PEOPLE
KNOW HOW TO
BREAK THE ICE.

SOME KNOW
HOW TO MELT IT.

YEARS ALONE
CANNOT
MEASURE HOW
MUCH ONE HAS
TRULY LIVED.

Anthony Burrill |
anthonyburrill.com

40 pages each, 210 x 210 mm (8¼ x 8¼ in) |

Book Smarts is a series of three books made by freelance designer Anthony Burrill in collaboration with writer Chad Rea. The idea for the books came out of a shared interest in the language of self-help books. These books are an antidote to the preachy language of regular self-help books. *Book Smarts #1, #2* and *#3* were released in 2005 in editions of 500 each.

*'I started work in the early 1990s after I left the Royal College of Art.
I have always produced my own products as part of my work; at first it was
cheaply produced photocopied books using minimal means and inexpensive materials.
This gave the work a "lo-fi" quality that I like.'*
Anthony Burrill

Brighten the Corners |
brightenthecorners.com

London- and Stuttgart-based design studio Brighten the Corners designed and published the children's book *Victor & Susie – He Came in the Vegetable Box* in 2008. *Victor & Susie* – a story about caring and letting go – was written and illustrated by Billy Kiosoglou with typography by Frank Philippin.

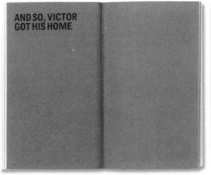

| 72 pages, 82 x 130 mm (3¼ x 5⅛ in)

36 pages, 140 x 100 mm (5½ x 3⅞ in)

'Both the commissioned work and my own books are part of what I like doing,
so I am happy doing both so that people can see different aspects of my work and
different ways of dealing with ideas.'
Iro Tsavala

Iro Tsavala |
iroillustration.gr

Recent Royal College of Art graduate Iro Tsavala is originally from Greece and based in London.

Opposite page: The image-based narrative book *The Party* was printed lithographically in two colours in an edition of 30. The original idea for the storyline was based on the short story *Light is Like Water* by Gabriel Garcia Marquez; two sentences from the original text are taken to be included in the book as pauses between the image sequences. The book creates a narrative based around the worlds of the imagination and daydream, where the real and unreal intermingle. *The Party* was created by Iro Tsavala with design contributions by Valerio Di Lucente.

This page: *Tick Tock* is a silent narrative in the form of a miniature book. It was digitally printed in an edition of 14.

Both books were hand-bound and completed in summer 2008.

| 25 pages, 80 x 90 mm (3⅛ x 3½ in)

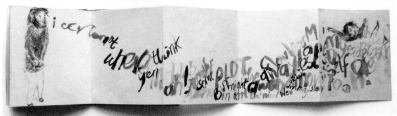

Sing Statistics | I Am The Friction

singstatistics.co.uk
eveningtweed.com
abouttoday.co.uk

Edinburgh-based Sing Statistics are graphic designer Jez
Burrows and illustrator Lizzy Stewart. Their first book, *I Am
The Friction* from 2008, is written by Burrows and illustrated by
Stewart. It has two covers and reads from both directions: one
half of the book is composed of stories inspired by illustrations,
while the other contains illustrations inspired by stories. It's a
beautiful, hand-bound book; a numbered, limited edition of
100; and both covers are four-colour Gocco printed.

24 pages, 127 x 191 mm (5 x 7½ in)

Ian Caulkett | Fantastic Suburbia

fantasticsuburbia.com
iancaulkett.net
tiptoecollective.co.uk

Ian Caulkett is a member of Tiptoe – a
London-based illustration collective he
formed with Mark Whittle and James
Nicholls in 2008.

Fantastic Suburbia is an independently
published collection of words (poems and
prose) and pictures (illustrations and designs)
originally created by Ian Caulkett and writer
Sarah Remy Lee, who are influenced by 1950s
and 1960s beat poetry and literature.

*'We never felt a desire to make money, apart from simply covering costs.
It has always been about sharing our passions with as many as people as we can.'*
Ian Caulkett, Fantastic Suburbia

Bureau l'Imprimante |
wmaker.net/imprimante
limprimante.myshopify.com

Paris – Normandie features cartographics of the late 1970s French punk scene, with important people and strategic places – both in Paris and Rouen, where Bureau l'Imprimante is based. It was designed and published by Loïc Boyer who set up Bureau l'Imprimante in 2001 as a non-profit organization to allow him to issue books and zines in small quantities.
Paris – Normandie is inspired by the work of Russian futurists Vasilii Kamenskii and Andrei Kravtsov. It was published in an edition of 60 using vintage wallpaper as stock with silkscreened artworks printed on the reverse side.

| 12 pages, 155 x 210 mm (6⅛ x 8¼ in)

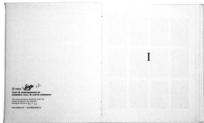

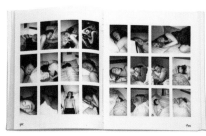

'My sideline projects not only inform my commissioned
work, but help direct me to what I want to do next.
They give me a chance to define my interests and develop new ideas.'

Kimberly Hall

Kimberly Hall |
nottene.net

Educated in fine arts at the School of the Museum of Fine Arts in Boston, and later receiving her MA in textiles at Central Saint Martins in the UK, Kimberly Hall works as a clothing and accessory designer, but also does freelance graphic design work and arts projects as well as her own self-initiated work.

Opposite page: The book *2001* was designed and produced by her, and written and photographed together with Justin Hardison. *2001* is a collection of photos and conversations created each day of that year. *2001* recounts milestones of that year in both personal struggles and world events, from weddings and births to the news in Afghanistan and on 9/11. The hand-sewn book is divided in half and opens from both the front and the back, when flipped upside down. *2001* was created in an edition of 100.

Right: The *Dream Book* is an illustrated account of one of Hall's recurring dreams with blank pages for the reader to fill in his or her own dreams. It was printed in a limited run (eight so far). The pages are laser printed on newsprint paper, soft-bound with hand-stitching, and covered in selvedge ends of found fabric – credited in each book. Each book is finished in a unique fabric.

Making Do |
makingdo.org.uk

Making Do is an independent publication and a collective with a focus on the methods of producing creative work. It is conceived, edited and designed by Andrea Francke, Mary Ikoniadou, Asli Kalinoglu and Alexandre Coco – three graphic designers and one fine artist – and is published in London. Some of the collective's members are employed full-time; others work independently and occasionally collaborate on commissioned design projects. They all work on the publication in their spare time.

Left: Issue 0, Making Do as a process for production of work.

Above: Issue 1, Translation as a method and an outcome.

Both issues were released in editions of 300.

*'Graphic design can be just a profession,
but for the truly successful it is often more than that.'*
Making Do

Musa |

musaworklab.com
nlfmagazine.com

Lisbon-based Musa was formed in 2003 by
Raquel Viana, Paulo Lima and Ricardo Alexandre.
Commercial work developed by MusaWorkLab
helped to put the Portuguese design scene firmly
on the map.

Above: In 2004 the collective of graphic designers
organized the 'MusaTour' exhibition supporting the
MusaBook project – the first Portuguese graphic
design book ever compiled (published in 2006 by
IdN, Hong Kong).

Below: Since 2003, the versatile collective has also
published art and graphics magazine *NLF – Nothing
Lasts Forever*. In 2007 they republished the first
eight *NLF* issues in book form in collaboration
with Basheer Graphic Books, Singapore.

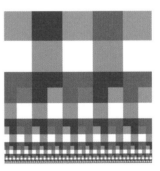

I RMX Extended Play, 2001

I RMX – A Visual Remix Project, 2000

*'The beginning of our product history is also the beginning of our collective history.
Rinzen formed as a direct consequence of collaborating on our first design remixing project.'*

Rinzen

| Fresh RMX, 2001, 3.6 m x 120 mm (11ft 8in x 4¾in)

Rinzen |
rinzen.com

Australian design and art collective Rinzen is best known for the collaborative approach of its five members, forming as a result of their visual and audio remix project, RMX. Extending the concept for their 2001 book, the group invited over 30 international participants to sequentially rework digital art, in what has now become a common method of collaboration among graphic designers and illustrators.

Opposite page, left: RMX one – eight players (all based in Brisbane, digital files swapped in person at weekly meetings), creating pieces on eight themes resulting in 64 visual remixes. Outcome: large perforated fold-out poster pack, remixed music CD, DIY critique stickers, exhibition invitations and poster, exhibitions in Brisbane and Berlin.

Opposite page, right: RMX two – 34 players (based all around the world, vector files swapped by email), creating pieces on six themes resulting in 96 visual remixes. Outcome: book published by DGV (Germany), exhibitions in Brisbane and Berlin, workshop in Hong Kong.

Above: 39 players (based all around the world, digital files swapped by email). The first participant produces a piece, with only the final edge being passed on to the next player. They must then continue the image, starting off from where it began. The end result is a panorama of chopping and changing images: different horizon lines, view-points, styles and worlds. Outcome: frieze, exhibition in Sydney.

Neighbourhood, 2004–6

Left, top to bottom:
Spätzle by Rilla Alexander, Rinzen, Australia
Erber by Friends With You, USA
Dougal by Jason Groves, Shynola, UK

Above, top to bottom:
Melville by Adrian Clifford, Rinzen, Australia
Merry Melville by Julian Gatto, Gaga Inc, USA
Mel by Colorblok, Argentina

*'There is no real divide between our products and our client work –
ideally they are all just realizations of our ideas and passions –
a chain of stylistic and thematic elements that are indelibly Rinzen.'*

Rinzen

| *10 Days in Sapporo*, 2007

Rinzen |
rinzen.com

Opposite page, top left: Rinzen's RMX four – *Neighbourhood*, 2004–6. Beginning with the blank canvas of a featureless cloth toy, a sequence of characters was born from the hands of the players, progressively reworking (or remaking) the hapless figures in a series of hands-on remixes. The 45 participants used a huge range of techniques to bring each stage to life – stitching, painting, drawing, tailoring, accessorizing; even adding, removing, or repurposing body parts – the severity of the changes being decided by the nimble hands of each player. Outcome: book published by Victionary, Hong Kong, exhibition and workshop at Pictoplasma Berlin 2005.

Above and right: RMX five – 10 Days in Sapporo; RMX Big Bang Workshop, 2007. Rinzen led 15 participants over ten days in the transformation of a room at the Intercross Creative Centre in Sapporo, Japan. Each day a different task was aimed at exploring the fundamentals of image creation. Outcome: painted room, workshop book published by ICC, Japan.

Alexander Egger |
satellitesmistakenforstars.com

Alexander Egger is an Italian-born Vienna-based graphic designer who has published his own series of zines entitled *Everybody get out of the pool* since 2007. All have the same format – 140 x 200 mm (5½ x 7⅞ in) – and are printed in black on 80 gsm laser copier paper in different colours. Each edition is 100 and none of them is signed or numbered – and there is no identification of the author.

List of zines published so far:
People who make noise are dangerous (48 pages)
Places to go, people to see, things to do (52 pages)
Many people would never fall in love
  if they didn't hear so much about it (36 pages)
In the long term we are all dead (36 pages)
Sex is nostalgia for sex
  when once it used to be exciting (36 pages)
But the sun likes me (36 pages)
Buildings, not homes (36 pages)
How can you smile while you talk bullshit (48 pages)
Drawing down (24 pages)
text = bad communication (28 pages)
1984 was an extremely boring year (40 pages)
Notes on unexpected feelings
  after the resumption of bodily relations (32 pages)
The top is just the bottom in reverse (36 pages)
Weather observations (24 pages)

'I find it extremely important for a designer to clearly take position and to use their communicative skills for social, cultural and political activities and not just to feed the market with another fancy product or trendy design.'
Alexander Egger

Alexander Egger |
satellitesmistakenforstars.com

Satellites Mistaken for Stars (this page) is the first monograph by graphic designer Alexander Egger, who edited and produced the book entirely by himself in 2005 before presenting it to potential publishers. Gingko Press launched it at the Frankfurt Book Fair in 2008.

Opposite page, top: *Scientists say until 1964 mankind will live permanently on the moon* is another book project by Egger.

Opposite page, bottom: *We have no scar to show for happiness* was edited and produced by Egger between 2007 and 2008. The title of the book is a quote by writer Chuck Palahniuk.

180 pages, 218 x 275 mm (8⅝ x 10¾ in) |

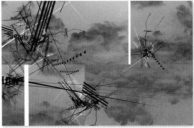

'*I am employed and sometimes work as a freelancer.
When I feel exhausted or unsatisfied I do my own work in long, sleepless nights.*'
Alexander Egger

220 pages, 210 x 280 mm (8¼ x 11 in)

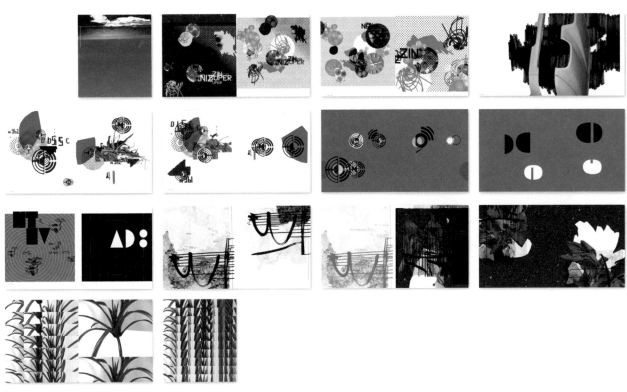

180 pages, 220 x 240 mm (8¾ x 9½ in)

Jeffrey Bowman and Andrew J. Miller |

The Wizard's Hat
thewizardshat.co.uk
mrbowlegs.co.uk
komadesign.co.uk

The Wizard's Hat is the outlet for collaborative collective Jeffrey Bowman and Andrew J. Miller. They have worked together since 2006 to produce work and products that celebrate their love of illustration, design and art, and the obsessive habit of doodling. The A5-size launch issue shown here was released in 2008.

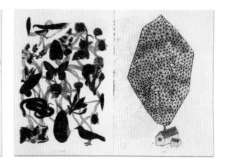

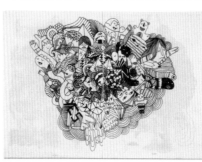

'It started once I'd established a tight group of friends at university, we pushed each other to do things individually and collaboratively taking things slightly more seriously. From then on making zines, badges, T-shirts and other items became a regular thing.'

Jeffrey Bowman, The Wizard's Hat

Zeptonn |
zeptonn.nl

Zeptonn is Jan Willem Wennekes, aka Stinger. He is based in the Netherlands, and works on his own illustration projects and collaborations with other artists.

Below: *Stingermania* from 2006 is the first publication by Groningen-based Zeptonn.

Right: *Black & White Freedrawings* from 2008 is a unique exploration of collaborative drawing. In the book, over 40 international artists collaborate on a drawing with Zeptonn. These collaborations are called 'freedrawings' to highlight the lack of restrictions, themes and guidelines. *Black & White Freedrawings* features over 160 illustrations and more than 100 photos. It comes with an additional yellow dustcover that can double as a poster, and is produced in an eco-friendly way.

I 132 pages, 210 x 297 mm (8¼ x 11¾ in)

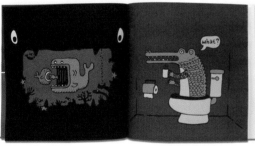

I 44 pages, 190 x 190 mm (7½ x 7½ in)

Nous Vous | Nous Vous Press
nousvous.eu

Pocket Sized is the first publication from 2007 by Nous Vous (We You), a British visual communications collective. It was litho-printed in black and white with a screen-printed cover in an edition of 500, and individually hand-bound. *Pocket Sized* was curated, edited and designed by Nous Vous Collective and Marc Alcock. Contributors are invited to respond to a given theme, the first issue's being 'Space'. Shown here are contributions by (from top to bottom) Thom Hudson/ Edmund Cook, Grandpeople, Nous Vous, Luke Best and Mark Howe.

The second issue is due to be published in 2009. The theme will be 'Future' and it will be in colour.

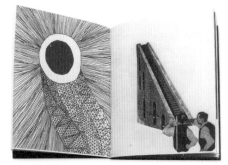

| 80 pages, 105 x 128 mm (4⅛ x 5 in)

'We produced Pocket Sized *because not many people were familiar with our work and we wanted to be featured next to our respected peers, and we couldn't see many ways of being in a book next to them if we didn't do it ourselves.'*

Nous Vous

Zeroten |
zeroten.net

Zeroten is a London-based freelance artist and illustrator. *Exoskeletor* from 2007 is his third zine and his favourite so far. He purposely chose not to restrict himself to a theme for this issue, enabling him to explore more freely and creatively. *Exoskeletor* was released in an edition of 40.

40 pages, 145 x 210 mm (5¾ x 8¼ in) |

Craig Atkinson | Café Royal
craigatkinson.co.uk
caferoyal.org

Reward by British artist Craig Atkinson is a collection of selected drawings from his sketchbook pages. It was published in 2008 by Café Royal – his family-run online shop and offline publishing house specializing in artists' books and zines. *Reward* was printed digitally in an edition of 250.

| 24 pages, 148 x 210 mm (5¾ x 8¼ in)

'Since I started as a freelance illustrator it has always been in my mind to build up
a variety of products for sale, that would both bring in a little extra cash
and help to promote my artwork.'

Joe Rogers, Colourbox

Joe Rogers, Colourbox |
colourboxonline.com
colourboxshop.bigcartel.com

Opposite page: Joe Rogers, aka Rudiger
the Illustrator, and his studio Colourbox
are based near Birmingham in the UK.
Featured here are some of the 24 cards
from Rogers' bound postcard book
Colour vs. Context. A limited edition of
500 stamped and numbered copies was
produced in 2008.

DGPH |
dgph.com.ar
molestown.com

Martin Lowenstein and Diego Vaisberg
run Argentinian design studio DGPH.
Molestown from 2006 is the first book
by the multi-disciplinary team. The book
features some of their first illustrations
after their launch in 2005 and also
includes short stories and profiles of
the characters. Its 64 illustrated pages
also feature a few guest artists including
Jeremyville, Acampante, Christopher
Lee and Human Empire. Molestown
was printed in an edition of 1,000.

Mike Perry |

midwestisbest.com
untitled-a-magazine.com

Mike Perry works in Brooklyn, New York. His first book, *Hand Job* from 2006, and his second book, *Over & Over* from 2008, were both published by Princeton Architectural Press and there are more books in the pipeline.

Right: *The Landscape Between Time and Space* was self-published for Mike Perry's 2008 solo show in London. It was printed four-colour offset on newspaper.

Opposite page: *It is a Circular Universe* – again printed in four-colour offset on newspaper – was self-published for Perry's art show in Silver Lake, Los Angeles in 2007.

| 16 pages, 267 x 419 mm (10½ x 16½in)

'Part of me thinks that it would be brilliant [to focus 100 per cent on self-initiated projects] but I often think that it might get boring after a while [without commissioned work].'
Mike Perry

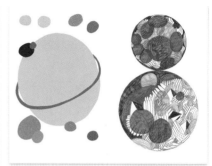

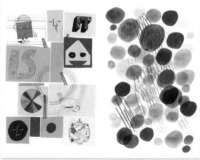

| 16 pages, 279 x 432 mm (11 x 17 in)

Mike Perry |
midwestisbest.com
untitled-a-magazine.com

Mike Perry launched his favourite self-published magazine *Untitled a…* in 2007. The idea of the magazine is very open and he wants *Untitled a…* to evolve from issue to issue.

This page: The fashion issue *Untitled 001* from 2007 was printed in two-colour offset.

Opposite page: The swimsuit edition *Untitled 002* was printed in three-colour offset in 2008.

| 96 pages, 152 x 229 mm (6 x 9 in)

'I had been doing my own publications from the beginning.
But in 2007 I stepped it up and founded Untitled *magazine.'*
Mike Perry

96 pages, 229 x 305 mm (9 x 12 in)

Vier5 | Fairy Tale

vier5.de
fairytale-magazine.com
vier5.de/fashiondepartment
v5-warehouse.com

The two Germans Marco Fiedler and
Achim Reichert and their Paris-based
design studio Vier5 launched their
bi-annual magazine *Fairy Tale* in 2003,
followed by the launch of the Vier5
fashion department and their own fashion
brand V5FD in 2008. *Fairy Tale* reflects on
fashion, photography, graphic design and
art. Each issue is dedicated to a certain
theme, is released with alternative covers,
and contains two booklets – one picture
book and one containing text.

Right and below: Issue #10, *Arcitectura
et Interiori* from 2008 and the Vier5 font
Nub-21 from 1998.

Opposite page: Vier5 custom typefaces
that are applied to self-initiated and
commissioned projects. *1Try*, *172Try-Reg*,
1722Try-Reg, *fliessbold* and *7Try-medserif*
are from 1995, *SnoopText-Roman* from
2004 and *Einfach-Medium* from 2008.

| 230 x 330 mm (9⅛ x 13 in)

'*Most of the products we create are originally independent projects
and afterwards we decide if we want to commercialize them.*'

Vier5

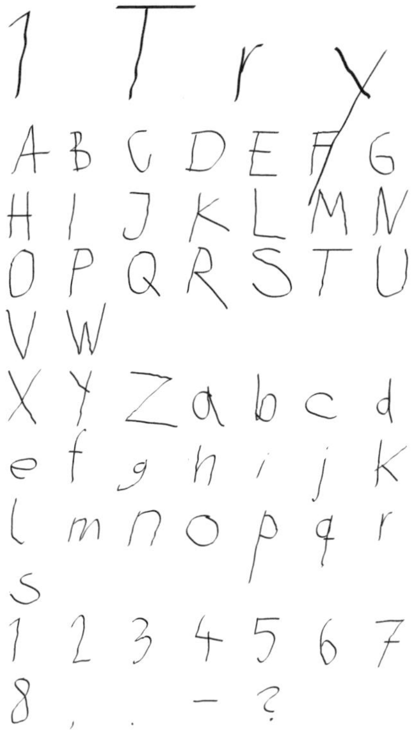

1 Try

A B C D E F G
H I J K L M N
O P Q R S T U
V W
X Y Z a b c d
e f g h i j k
l m n o p q r
s
1 2 3 4 5 6 7
8 , . - ?

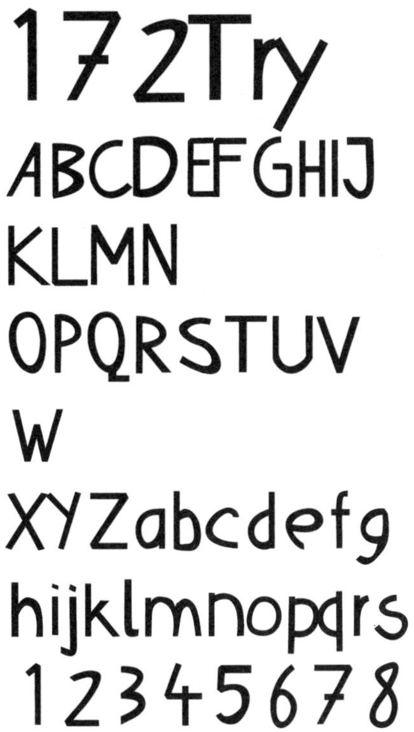

172Try

ABCDEFGHIJ
KLMN
OPQRSTUV
W
XYZabcdefg
hijklmnopqrs
12345678

Snoop

ABCDEFGHIJ
KLMN
OPQRSTUVW
XYZabcdefg
hijklmnopq
rs12345
678,.-?
ffffffffffffffffffff

1722Try

ABCDEFGHIJ
KLMN
OPQRSTUV
W
XYZabcdefg
hijklmnopqrs
12345678

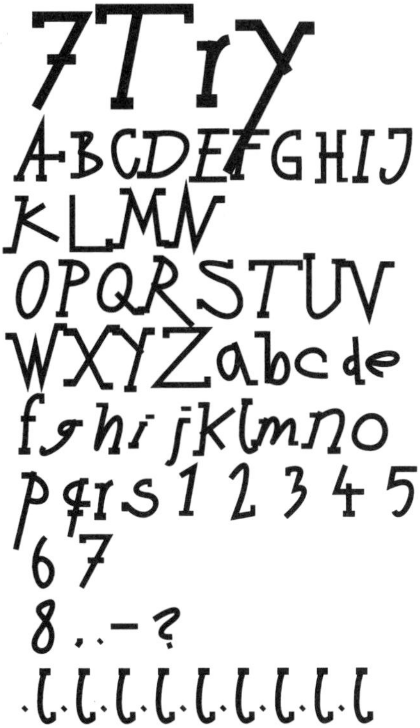

7Try

ABCDEFGHIJ
KLMN
OPQRSTUV
WXYZabcde
fghijklmno
pqrs12345
67
8,.-?
͡͡͡͡͡͡͡͡͡͡͡͡

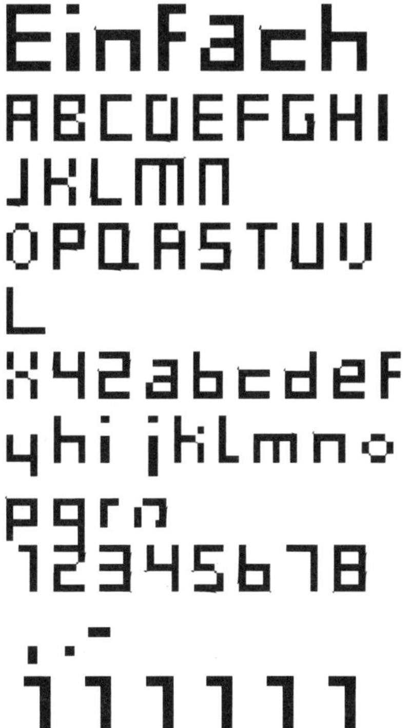

Einfach

ABCDEFGHI
JKLMN
OPQRSTUV
L
X42abcdef
yhijklmno
pqrn
12345678
.,-
1111111

'It's very refreshing and motivating if your way of working and the things you do are diverse.'
Martin Lorenz, Twopoints.Net

Twopoints.Net | The One Weekend Book Projects

twopoints.net
theoneweekendbookseries.com

Barcelona-based design studio Twopoints.Net, founded in 2000, is run by German graphic designer Martin Lorenz and his wife Lupi Asensio.

They launched *The One Weekend Book Series* in 2003. Since then, Lorenz has travelled to cities like Berlin, Copenhagen, Milan, New York City, The Hague and Barcelona to make 48-page books with different artists in only one weekend. Back home, he and Asensio hand-produced 50 copies of each book, which were then distributed and sold worldwide.

A 300-page compilation of the first five volumes was published in collaboration with Spanish publisher Actar in 2006.

Calin Kruse | dienacht
dienacht-magazine.com

Romanian-born graphic designer and photographer Calin Kruse is based in Trier, Germany. In 2006 he launched a small photocopied artzine, *Rough*, and since 2007 he has also been designer and editor of *dienacht* – a full-colour magazine on photography, design and subculture. Bilingual (German and English) *dienacht* is self-published biannually in an edition of 1,000 individually numbered copies.

Right: *dienacht*, issue 3 from April 2008, cover and sample spreads.

Below, left to right: *Rough* #1 by Kruse and Jannette Mensch, *Rough* #2 by Kruse and Maurice Vink and *Rough* #3 by Kruse and Therese Pohl. Each was published in editions of 50.

Bottom: Sample spread from *Rough* #1.

124 pages, 150 x 180 mm (5⅛ x 7⅛ in)

105 x 148 mm (4⅛ x 5¾ in)

'I always wanted to produce a really independent magazine, without any publishing house or someone else who would tell me what I can do and what I can't.'

Calin Kruse, dienacht

Supersentido |
supersentido.cl

Artist and designer Pablo 'Pece' Castro, aka Supersentido, is based in Santiago, Chile. He started his project *La Nueva Galerìa de Bolsillo* (*LNGB*) – the new pocket gallery – in 2005. This foil-blocked slipcase contains ten pocket magazines compiled and produced by Supersentido, featuring his own work and that of nine other hand-picked street artists. Single issues were released in an edition of 250 each and the complete set with slipcase was published in 2006 in an edition of 100. Samples shown here are from volumes two and seven, entitled *Color PC* and *Solol
gos* respectively.

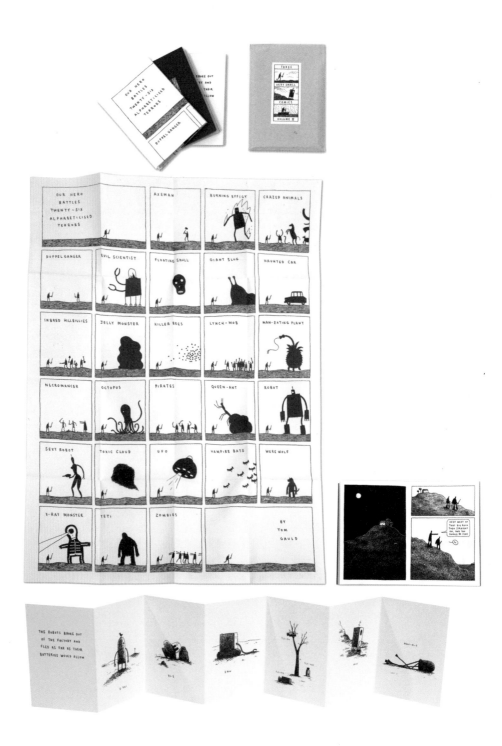

'My commercial work and my self-published work have always gone hand in hand. I began self-publishing while at the RCA and the comics I made there were a big part of my original portfolio.'

Tom Gauld, Cabanon Press

I Folded, 88 x 122 mm (3½ x 4¾ in)

Tom Gauld | Cabanon Press
cabanonpress.com

Scottish-born, London-based freelance illustrator and cartoonist Tom Gauld writes, draws and designs comic books, some of which are published through Cabanon Press, an imprint he has run with Simone Lia since 2001 when they both graduated from the Royal College of Art. Shown here are volumes two and three of his *Three Very Small Comics* from 2004 and 2007 respectively.

Opposite page: Volume two, the poster *Our Hero Battles Twenty-six Alphabeticised Terrors*, the booklet *Invasion* and the concertina fold *The Robots Broke Out Of The Factory And Fled As Far As Their Batteries Would Allow*.

Above: Volume three, the poster *The Gauld Collection – Case W (misc)*, the booklet *Gardening* and the concertina fold *The Art Of War*.

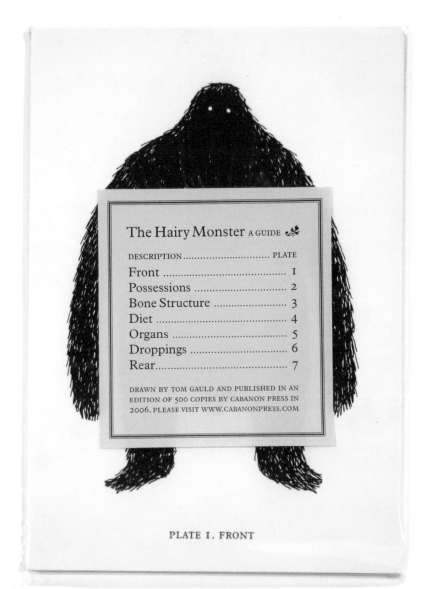

PLATE I. FRONT

Tom Gauld | Cabanon Press
cabanonpress.com

The Hairy Monster – A Guide was drawn by illustrator and cartoonist Tom Gauld and published in an edition of 500 by his imprint, Cabanon Press, in 2006.

The Hairy Monster A GUIDE

DESCRIPTION	PLATE
Front	I
Possessions	2
Bone Structure	3
Diet	4
Organs	5
Droppings	6
Rear	7

DRAWN BY TOM GAULD AND PUBLISHED IN AN EDITION OF 500 COPIES BY CABANON PRESS IN 2006. PLEASE VISIT WWW.CABANONPRESS.COM

Folded, 105 x 148 mm (4⅛ x 5¾ in)

TOM GAULD, 433/500

'A lot of my illustration work comes from people who like the comics, and conversely a lot of things in my self-published works come from ideas and techniques which began in my commercial work.'

Tom Gauld, Cabanon Press

Jon Burgerman and Sune Ehlers | Hello Duudle

helloduudle.com
jonburgerman.com
duudle.dk

Hello Duudle, from 2004, was the first book UK artist Jon Burgerman made in collaboration with Danish artist Sune Ehlers. The concertina book folds out to approximately 1.5 m in length (4ft 11in) and is printed with hidden spot UV doodles and a sheet of stickers. On the reverse of the colourful frieze are little character biographies introducing the reader to the world of *Hello Duudle*.

In 2006 the team made a follow-up book called *Hello Duudle: The Duudleville Tales*. The format was similar but this time it came in a gold-foiled art box, and was accompanied by stickers and a numbered and signed drawn Duudle by either Ehlers or Burgerman. The edition was limited to 1,000 copies.

| Unfolded, 1,010 x 175 mm (39¾ x 6⅞ in)

Stills from *Trans-it* CD-ROM

View from FL@33's first studio (a flat #33) |

'Self-initiated FL@33 projects, such as our sound collection bzzzpeek.com, our online boutique stereohype.com or Trans-form magazine helped us to find many of the clients we are still working with today.'
Agathe Jacquillat and Tomi Vollauschek, FL@33

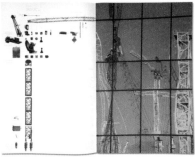

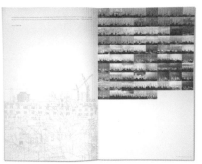

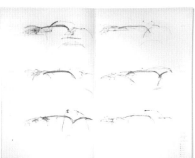

FL@33 | Stereohype

flat33.com
stereohype.com
trans-port.org

Trans-form, Trans-it, trans-port.org is a self-initiated architecture, art and design publication from FL@33 founders Agathe Jacquillat and Tomi Vollauschek. This award-winning first issue is a conceptual project, based on an everyday observation of tower cranes, comprising a magazine, a CD-ROM and a website.

The project was made public in July 2001 during the Royal College of Art Masters' degree show in London. The large-scale magazine explores the magic of urban sculptures that appear and disappear in the cities we live in. Tower cranes that are lifting, transporting, reconstructing, drawing, cutting, performing and 'transforming' are usually unnoticed by the public. *Trans-form* presents information about tower cranes and crane operators' daily work in the sky. The attached CD-ROM adds videos and animations combining industrial structures with natural imagery and presents a cityscape metamorphosis, portraying our cities as being in a 'larval stage'. Trans-port.org offers you the possibility to 'build your own crane', to 'climb the crane' and to 'be a crane operator'.

Trans-form was self-published in an edition of 1,000. It was printed on uncoated stock and wire stitched. A few remaining copies of the award-winning *Trans-form* magazine are available exclusively at stereohype.com.

| 320 x 500 mm (12⅝ x 19¾ in)

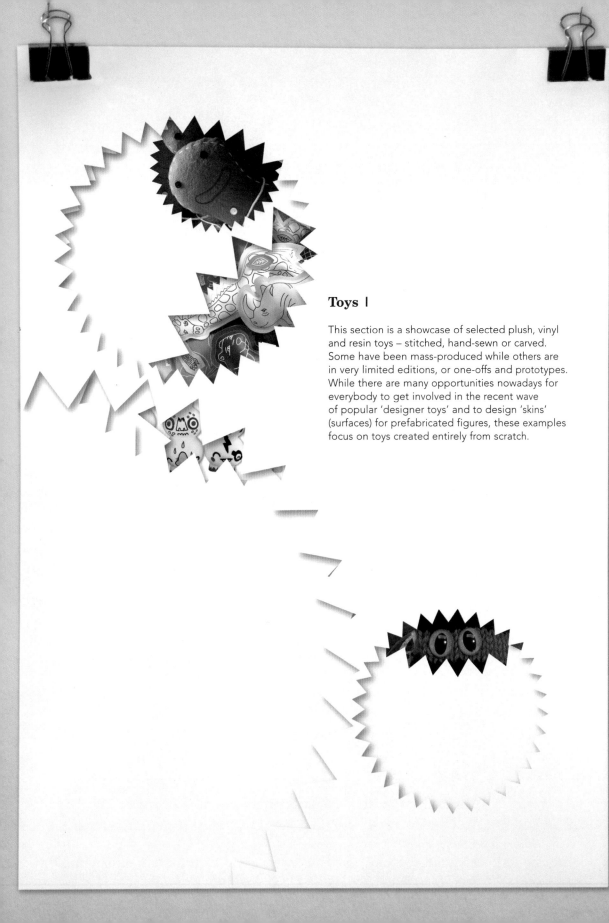

Toys |

This section is a showcase of selected plush, vinyl and resin toys – stitched, hand-sewn or carved. Some have been mass-produced while others are in very limited editions, or one-offs and prototypes. While there are many opportunities nowadays for everybody to get involved in the recent wave of popular 'designer toys' and to design 'skins' (surfaces) for prefabricated figures, these examples focus on toys created entirely from scratch.

Plushood |
plushood.com

Plushood is a series of plush dolls with five amazing characters, created by industrial designer Shlomi Schillinger and illustrator, designer and animator Tamar Moshkovitz (also known as TAM). The Plushoods are called Joske, Dolores, Miss Moss, Vigo and Pinto and are made of soft and colourful fleece fabric, while the face and bottom parts are made of vinyl (leather imitation) fabric with silkscreen-printed graphics. The dolls are all handmade in Israel.

I Approximate size: 340 x 240 mm (13⅜ x 9½ in)

'Shlomi called me one day and asked me if I wanted to make dolls. He's an industrial designer and was looking for an illustrator and designer. He saw my website and wanted to collaborate with me.'

TAM, Plushood

Airside | Airside Shop

airside.co.uk
airsideshop.com
brassier.blogspot.com

The Stitches are woolly creatures looked after by Anne Brassier and Airside until new homes can be found for them. They arrive at Airside somewhat damaged, but will say very little about their previous lives. Airside rehabilitates them and finds new families for the Stitches to go and live with. Anne Brassier has been at London-based design studio Airside since 2001 and handles all press, marketing and new business matters. Anne is mother to the Stitches – woolly creatures adopted into new homes via Airside's online shop. They are approximately 140–200 mm tall (5½–7 ⅞ in).

FRAGILE

Adoption Certificate

JOHN STITCH

is hereby given in adoption,

on the 28 AUGUST 2005

Date of birth: 30th January 2005
Place of birth: London, England
Sex: Stitch

The above-mentioned has been adopted by

JOHN DOE

Resident of LONDON

BOYS BE AMBITIOUS

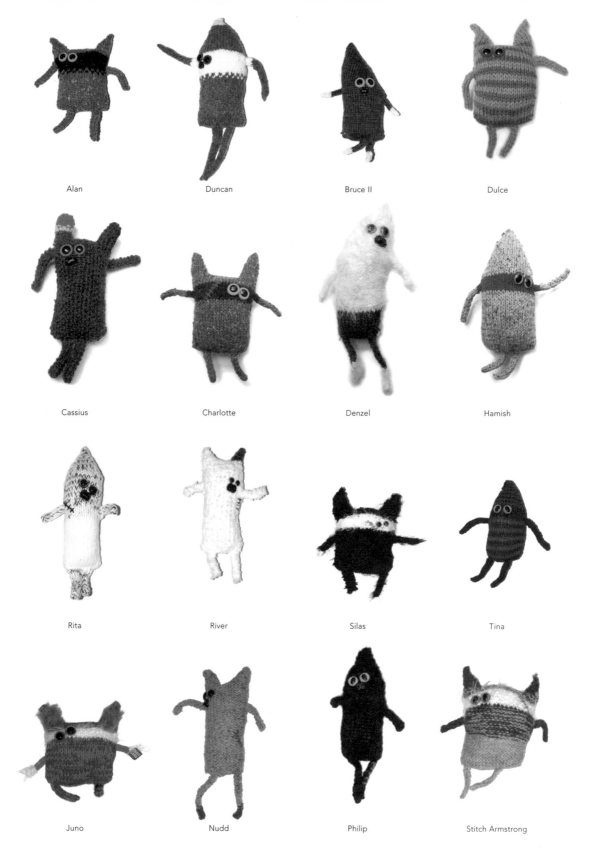

Alan

Duncan

Bruce II

Dulce

Cassius

Charlotte

Denzel

Hamish

Rita

River

Silas

Tina

Juno

Nudd

Philip

Stitch Armstrong

'Sometimes our clients laugh at the Stitches, although we would prefer them to laugh with the Stitches as some of them are quite fragile emotionally. The Stitches, that is…'

Anne Brassier, Airside

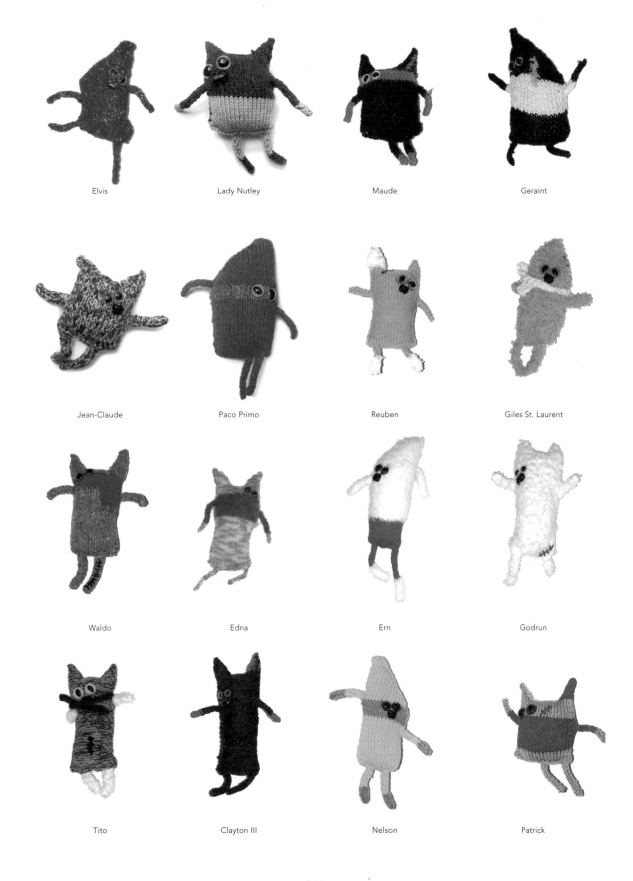

Elvis

Lady Nutley

Maude

Geraint

Jean-Claude

Paco Primo

Reuben

Giles St. Laurent

Waldo

Edna

Ern

Godrun

Tito

Clayton III

Nelson

Patrick

127 mm (5 in)

152 mm (6 in)

'Part of our philosophy is to release at least one self-initiated project per year.'
Diego Vaisberg, DGPH

DGPH |

dgph.com.ar
molestown.com

Opposite page, top: The *Topo* (mole) character by Argentinian design team DGPH was released in 2007 in collaboration with Hong Kong-based adFunture Workshop. The mole character was one of the first characters DGPH created after launching their studio in 2005 and it is the first they transformed into a vinyl toy. *Topo* was produced in three different colourways and there is also a blank version for people to customize themselves.

Opposite page, bottom: *Tsuchi* is one of the latest DGPH vinyl toys, this time made in collaboration with Munky King, Los Angeles. The figure represents one of the Molestown Gods – from the world created by DGPH. Presented at the San Diego Comic-Con 2008, there are four colourways, including a silver statue version and a special black-on-black version.

Left, top and middle: *Bubble Mole* is an inflatable toy from 2007 that was entirely produced, screen-printed and released by DGPH in a (now sold out) limited edition of 200. A special *Bubble Mole* edition of 100 units was also made for the DGPH USA Tour – an exhibition at Munky King Store in 2007. Also shown here is a customized wood-effect version of *Bubble Mole*, not yet released.

Left, bottom: This plush toy from 2007 is entitled *Cabello* and was made with eight different fabric textures, embroidery and screen-printing. It was developed in collaboration with Hicalorie, UK and with production assistance from Bigshot Toyworks. A total of 600 units were made – 300 original, 100 in black for Rotofugi, 100 in pink for *Clutter* magazine and 100 for Toyqube.

305 mm (12 in)

279 mm (11 in)

Kate Sutton |

katesutton.co.uk
katesutton.etsy.com

Kate Sutton has been working as a
freelance illustrator for the last few
years. Her line drawings and plush
creatures are often described as
whimsical. All her sideline products
are lovingly hand-crafted.

Right: There is a whole heap of different
monsters knitted by Kate over the years.
They all have slight differences – even if
it's just longer arms.

Opposite page, top: *The One That Got
Away* is a scrumptious series of plush
gingerbread men – some only miss a limb
while others are missing half of their head.

Opposite page, bottom: *Pirate Pigeons*
were among the first toys Sutton made
to sell in 2003 and she still makes the
odd one today. The *Pirate Vegetables*
and *Tea Set* were made for a plush food
exhibition in the US. They are all one-offs,
except for the carrots and peas, which she
has continued to make and sell.

250 mm (9⅞ in) |

*'Even if I had a range of manufactured products on the market
I would continue to make small runs / limited edition items as I love all things
handmade and it's just part of what I do.'*
Kate Sutton

 200 mm (7⅞ in)

 200 mm (7⅞ in)

 150–350 mm (5⅞–13¾ in)

 life-size

TADO and Jon Burgerman | collaboration

tado.co.uk
jonburgerman.com

These two projects were created for a collaborative show in Paris in 2007 entitled 'Immature Miniatures'. Sheffield-based illustration pair Mike and Katie of TADO teamed up with UK artist Jon Burgerman to create these beautiful pieces.

Right: Hand-sewn and printed felt plush with doodles by Jon Burgerman and TADO. These plushes were lovingly hand-sewn by Marion Hawkes and measure approximately 260 x 160 mm (10¼ x 6⁵⁄₁₆ in).

Opposite page: Hand-cast resin figures with doodles by Jon Burgerman and TADO. The figures were cast in the TADO-Kitchen and measure 75 x 40 mm (2⅞ x 1⁹⁄₁₆ in).

Most of our business (the bill-paying type!) comes from advertising and illustration, but we always keep ourselves busy with a lot of personal and collaborative projects.'

Mike and Katie, TADO

Bear Shroom, 254 mm (10 in)

TADO |
tado.co.uk

Hand-carved solid wooden figures from 2008 designed by
TADO and carved by Nick Hunter for TADO's solo exhibition,
'Lily: The Littlest Cannibal in Toronto'. The figures are made
from oak, lime and pine.

Tadomites, 102 mm (4 in) |

*'Products have always been right at the heart of what we wanted to do.
We love collecting other people's design-junk and love making our own even more!'*
Mike and Katie, TADO

Hermit, 279 mm (11 in)

Lily and Moon, 203 mm (8 in)

Happypets | Happypets Products
happypets.ch

Patrick 'Patch' Monnier, Violène Pont and Cédric Henny set up Happypets in 2000 – an experimental lab in the creative, graphic design, image and illustration domain, based in Lausanne, Switzerland. Their first vinyl designer toy, entitled *Rust*, was released in 2005 in a (now sold out) edition of 500. The character was created by selecting several big corporate logos (including Shell and Firestone), breaking them up into basic elements and reassembling them into this impressive character.

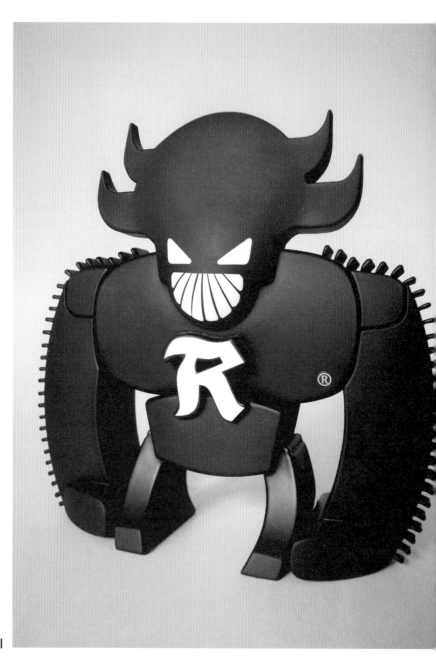

150 x 150 mm (6 x 6 in)

'As designers we aim to obscure the borders between traditional design practice and other fields, exploring different non-virtual media, creating and producing our own content such as clothes, toys, music, posters, editions and multi-use and multi-content objects.'

Patch, Happypets

TADO |
tado.co.uk

Handmade cashmere crochet and knit plush and felt plush with accents. Both were designed by TADO's Mike and Katie and, like the figures featured on pages 74 and 75, these too were created for the 2008 'Lily: The Littlest Cannibal...' solo show in Toronto. The elephant and octopus characters by TADO were hand-knitted by GranGran and the felt plush here on the left was hand-sewn by Kipi Kapopo.

| 178–279 mm (7–11 in)

| 508 mm (20 in)

Swigg Studio | Swigg Products!
thisisswigg.com

Stephanie Wenzel is a graphic artist living and working in Brooklyn, New York. In 2004 she founded Swigg Studio, a multi-discipline design firm, as well as Swigg Products!, which creates tactile goods for human enjoyment.

Right: *Swigg Critters* (including *Beverly the Beaver*, *Ricky the Rhino* and *Harold the Giraffe*) are made of vinyl materials which are animal-friendly and easy to clean. They are stuffed with poly-fill as well as poly-pellets for weight. The indentifying graphics are silkscreened onto fronts, backs and appliqués. Depending on the character, they measure approximately 178 x 330 mm (7 x 13 in).

Below: These *Fungi Sculpture* toys are weighted sculptures that can be used as a balancing tool for kids, or as part of a fungi forest inhabited by *Swigg Critters*. They are about 0.45 kg (1½ lb) each and measure approximately 178 x 178 mm (7 x 7 in).

'What I decided to do was to keep it small, experimental and limited as it had been in the beginning, which allowed passion about the ideas and excitement about the creation process to regenerate.'

Stephanie Wenzel, Swigg

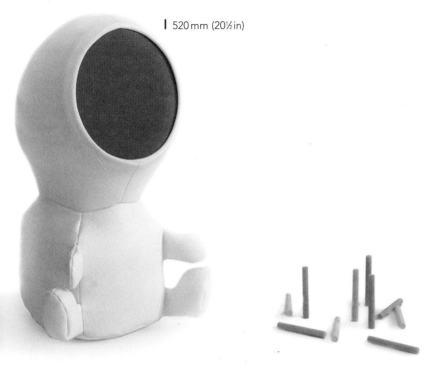

520 mm (20½ in)

Home de Caramel |
homedecaramel.com

Marc Esteban, Jordi Matosas and Oriol Rello are the founders of multi-disciplinary studio Home de Caramel, which created these prototypes of customizable toys.

Left: *Blackboard Kid* is a soft toy without a face. Instead of the face there is a blackboard, so that faces can be drawn on with the chalks that are supplied.

Below: *MuddlePuzzle Worm* is a plush toy that comes in separate pieces. Each module has hidden magnets on each side so elements can be freely attached to each other.

160 x 220 mm (6⁵⁄₁₆ x 8⁵⁄₈ in) and 200 x 300 mm (7⅞ x 11⅞ in)

Lunartik JOnes |
lunartik.com
lunartikshop.bigcartel.com

British artist Matt Jones, aka Lunartik JOnes, is best known for the conceptual art toy *Lunartik In A Cup Of Tea* (LIACOT).

Above: Taking a break and having a lovely cup of tea is a part of good old English heritage and the toy LIACOT is designed to reflect English eccentricity and the nation's love for tea-drinking. These hand-cast resin figures feature a toy sitting in a cup of tea, a shiny spoon and two sugar cubes.

Right, top: The *Bunny Custom* is one of 27 handmade customs. It features 18 tiny bunnies, a green tree and an orange carrot.

Right: *Mr Tea Custom* is the winner of the 2007 *Design A Lovely Cup Of Tea* competition, which Lunartik JOnes initiated. People from around the world submitted designs for this competition, using the Lunartik toy as their canvas. The winning design was then produced by Lunartik himself as a one-off piece and given to the competition winner David Jakes.

Opposite page, top: *The Self Army* is a toy designed to look like a miniature replica of Lunartik. The toy comes in many forms and has key features such as a chest logo, plug socket on the rear, artist jeans, a heart on the sleeve and box for a head.

I 160 mm (6⅚ in)

'Having an idea is all well and good but actually making it a reality, a physical object, is such an amazing feeling.'
Matt Jones, Lunartik JOnes

I *The Self Army* by Lunartik JOnes, 76 mm (3 in)

I 200 mm (7⅞ in)

Supersentido I
supersentido.cl

Pablo 'Pece' Castro, aka Supersentido, is a designer and illustrator based in Santiago, Chile. His work has been exhibited and published across Latin America and Europe. He designs garments and T-shirts, loves street art and art toys, and created this prototype of his first toy in 2008 for the Pictoplasma conference in Argentina. His wooden toy is called *Quesito* (cheese wedge).

Posters, Prints and Canvases |

Many of the selected projects in this chapter might
not even have been produced if the artists and
designers didn't have access to printing facilities,
as many of the featured posters and prints are hand-
printed – whether by screen-print or letterpress. This
hands-on approach is quite different to increasingly
popular digital print techniques – namely, high-quality
giclée print, digital prints on photo-paper or file-to-
canvas transfers – that enable studios and individuals
to offer on-demand artworks or the very small
editions that are also featured here.

'*It seems like more and more designers are feeling the need to let their artistic side out, and produce self-initiated work that's somewhere between art and design.*'

Eivind Søreng Molvær

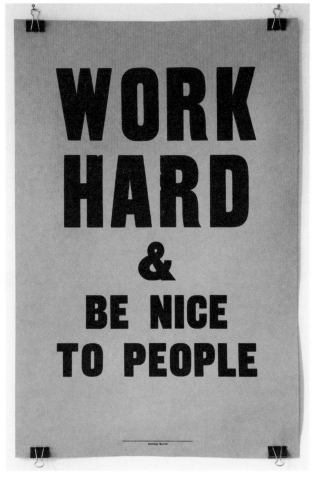

Eivind Søreng Molvær |
eivindmolvaer.com

London-based Eivind Søreng Molvær was born in
Norway where he studied before moving to London
in 2005 to attend the BA graphic design course at
Central Saint Martins. He graduated from there in 2008.
He screen-printed *The Italic Poster* in white on 140 gsm
black paper in an edition of 100. It was not initially
intended to be sold but due to high demand he started
offering this extraordinary poster on his website.

Anthony Burrill |
anthonyburrill.com

Royal College of Art (London) graduate Anthony
Burrill works as a freelance designer producing print,
moving image and interactive design based on direct
communication, in which humour often plays a central
role. He regularly creates self-initiated projects like his
best-selling posters *Work Hard & Be Nice To People*
and *It Is OK For Me To Have Everything I Want*. The
posters are produced using a traditional wood-block
letterpress process.

| *Early Bird* by Spencer Wilson

| *Sound in Print* by Miles Donovan

'We've always seen our products as a means of self-promotion rather than as a way of making money. We've actually been commissioned lots of times for commercial work after people have seen our products and books.'

Miles Donovan, Peepshow

| *Set Sail* by Luke Best | *Music Machine* by Andrew Rae | *House* by Lucy Vigrass

Peepshow | Peepshop
peepshow.org.uk
peepshop.org.uk

The product range by the ten-strong Peepshow collective is available from their own online shop and includes the five prints featured here. They are A2-size giclée prints on 100 per cent cotton 255 gsm paper. Each is in a limited edition of 30, signed and numbered by the artist.

FREE
TIME*

* WHILE STOCKS LAST

'I think clients are generally more interested in non-commissioned work, perhaps because no other company has used that particular style or idea.'
James Joyce, One Fine Day

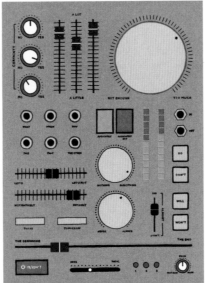

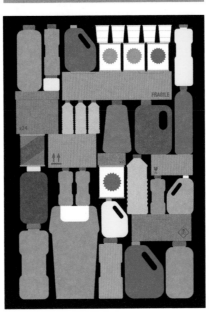

James Joyce, One Fine Day |
one-fine-day.co.uk

James Joyce is a London-based artist and designer. In 2006 he founded his own studio One Fine Day where he produces limited edition prints of his work as well as taking on commissions from international clients. His first solo gallery exhibition, 'Drawings And Other Objects', in London's Kemistry Gallery took place in 2008 and featured a selection of personal and commissioned images. Shown here are some of his screen-prints and giclée prints and, opposite, a picture of the exhibition.

I Shot the Sheriff

Words and Music by Bob Marley, 1974
89bpm
04 Mins 22 Secs

I Detail

Stuart Tolley, Transmission I Show Below
thisistransmission.com
showbelow.co.uk

Brighton-based graphic designer Stuart Tolley founded his design studio, Transmission, in 2008.

Tolley, together with a few illustrators, launched 'Show Below' – an annual contemporary art exhibition – in 2007. The work created for 'Show Below' is born out of the desire to experiment and not be restricted by corporate guidelines. His work often takes the form of mixed-media typographic posters. Work is sold through the exhibition in Brighton, UK, and online.

Detail I

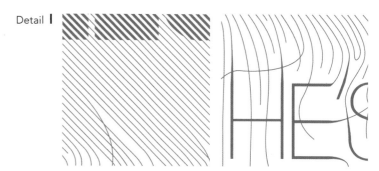

'I was lucky enough to meet some like-minded people and we decided to start exhibiting experimental work. This has developed into a regular exhibition called "Show Below".'
Stuart Tolley, Transmission

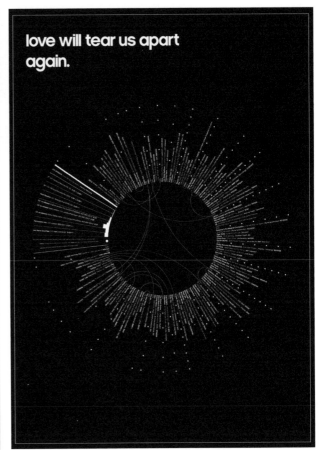

love will tear us apart
again.

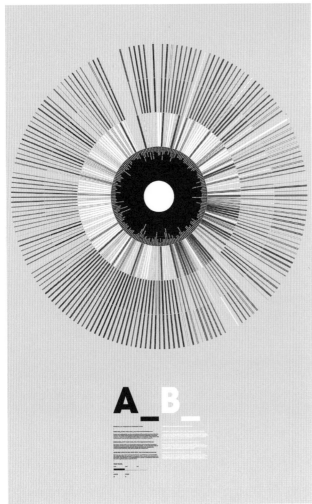

A_B_

Peter Crnokrak, The Luxury of Protest |
theluxuryofprotest.com

Croatian-born London-based Peter Crnokrak studied biology
and genetics before switching to graphic design. Crnokrak
works with Nick Bell Design but also does freelance work as
The Luxury of Protest (formerly ±). His self-initiated projects are
best characterized as design-informed art. In most cases they are
information visualization projects – computational aesthetics –
but also include object projects.

Above: *Love Will Tear Us Apart Again*. Using information design
principles and graphical techniques, the 85+ recorded covers of
Joy Division's 'Love Will Tear Us Apart' are mapped in relation to
the original recordings by the band.

Left: *A_B_ peace & terror etc. The computational aesthetics of
love & hate*. A_B... is a geopolitical survey of the 192 member
states of the United Nations with regard to the quantitative
degree to which each contributes to peace and terror in the
world. The screen-printed poster is double-sided with the A-side
(peace) printed verso in black and the B-side (terror) printed
recto in grey on a semi-translucent paper stock.

Jez Burrows |
eveningtweed.com
singstatistics.co.uk

Edinburgh-based graphic designer Jez
Burrows is a freelancer and a member of
Sing Statistics and the collective Evening
Tweed. He launched *The Modern
Listener's Guide* in 2008. It began as a
final-year university brief that took on
a life of its own once he graduated. His
series of large-format screen-prints marry
indie rock and information graphics.
Destroyer's Rubies by Destroyer was the
first album to be treated for the series.

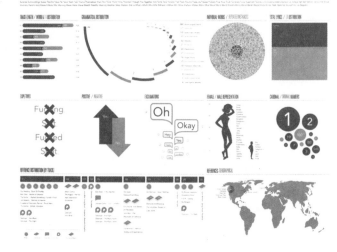

| Detail

'*The series definitely feels like quite a separate pursuit to commissioned work.
It's not often that commissions involve work based on music I love with no outside
art direction and no fixed deadline, so it's pretty liberating.*'

Jez Burrows

Genoa-based studio Artiva Design, run
by Daniele De Batté and Davide Sossi
created *Between the Lights* – a digitally
printed canvas – in 2008 (left). The canvas,
800 x 800 mm (31½ x 31½ in), is part of a
series of light-inspired pieces that are all
available from their online shop.

Below: *Composition No. 02* is part of
an ongoing series of one-off handmade
paper collages. Layers of cut paper and
card create pieces with sculptural and
architectural qualities.

Revenge is Sweet |
revengeissweet.org

Angelique Piliere from France and Lee Owens from Australia met while studying design in Australia and now live and work together in London where they set up Revenge is Sweet in 2007. After working in various London studios, Revenge is Sweet now produce work under their own name, crossing the lines between illustration, design and typography.

Wild Print (top left) was produced for the 'Blisters On My Fingers' exhibition by Print Club London, B2, silkscreen pink, silver and black, edition of 35.

Love & Hate (top, middle and right) is a hand-drawn typographic piece. A2, silkscreen gold and black/pink and black, limited edition.

Kill Me Softly (middle row) series of three spaghetti western theme prints. A2, silkscreen gold and black, edition of 60.

Schitzophrenic Circus (bottom row) series of three prints based on prostitute calling cards from London telephone boxes. A2, silkscreen gold and black, edition of 60.

'Our motivation for setting up Revenge is Sweet was to use it as a creative outlet. Something we can do without the restrictions of client-based or studio-based work.'

Angelique Piliere and Lee Owens, Revenge is Sweet

HudsonBec | If You Could

hudsonbec.com
ifyoucould.co.uk

Every month of 2008, HudsonBec released two new screen-prints: one from an established artist and one from an emerging artist through their *If You Could* project. The two-colour, limited edition screen-prints were available to buy only from the *If You Could* website for the duration of the month that they were released. This created unique editions, determined by the amount purchased. Contributors included Rob Ryan (left), Geneviève Gauckler (bottom left), Tom Gauld (bottom right) and many others – all responding to the question, 'If you could do anything tomorrow, what would it be?'.

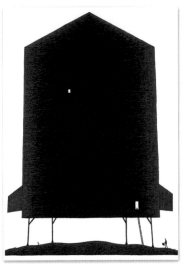

| B2, 655 x 480 mm (25¾ x 18⅞ in)

3 COLOUR MONSTER

'I quickly realized that I could make sure potential clients remembered me by giving them something that was screen-printed by hand — but even better than that, I could sell it to them and make some money, too.'
Andy Smith

Andy Smith |
asmithillustration.com

These hand screen-printed posters by British artist Andy Smith are based on characters from his sketch books or are experiments with typography that use some of the slogans or lines of speech that he notes down and collects. They are all made in editions of about 50 prints.

Jeremyville |
jeremyville.com

Jeremyville is an artist, product designer and animator who divides his time between his studios in Sydney and New York City. He screen-printed the two A1-sized prints *Central Park* and *New York City* in editions of 100 each. They were produced for a solo show at the Showroom Gallery, East Village, New York.

Al Heighton |
alanheighton.co.uk

British artist, designer and illustrator Al Heighton produced the two screen-prints *Bird and Some Pop* and *Flower Day* in 2008.

'Along with juggling commercial projects I think it's healthy to have a sideline to dip in to. Producing some prints may entertain, stimulate and win over an audience who want to buy into, own and collect.'
Al Heighton

123Klan |
123klan.com
123klan.bigcartel.com

Scien and Klor have been graffiti artists since 1989. 123Klan were the first to blend graffiti writing and graphic art. Formerly based in France, they now live and work in Montréal, Canada, where they continue their creative mix of commissioned and self-initiated projects. The two 123Klan posters shown here were created in 2008 in collaboration with Montréal's Yves Laroche Gallery.

DGPH |
dgph.com.ar
molestown.com

Argentinian design team DGPH releases a new line of prints every year. These two screen-printed posters belong to the 'Happy Villains' series, produced for an exhibition with the same name, that took place in 2008 at the Pixie Gallery Store in Taipei. Both prints were produced at A4 size with two-colour versions for each design in an edition of 40 per colourway. They were all signed and numbered.

Simon Wild |
simonwild.com
simonwild.bigcartel.com

Simon Wild is an artist and illustrator from
Suffolk, UK. His working methods include
collage, digital and screen-printing.
Grindavik Powerstation, *Northern Lights*
and *Reykjavik Red House* (top to bottom)
form a series of three signed, A4-size,
limited-edition prints. The series was
inspired by a road trip around Iceland and
each design is an attempt to explore what
is undoubtedly a unique, magical and
culturally inspiring country. The drawings
were initially created using simple pen
and ink and were then scanned and
coloured in Photoshop. They were
digitally printed on 188gsm fine-art
photo rag paper.

*'If, as a designer, you can turn your hand to a variety of disciplines then you are more likely
to find work. I believe this approach has opened up the breeding ground of designers' sidelines
so that they can successfully showcase their skills to a broader market.'*

Simon Wild

Jon Burgerman |
jonburgerman.com

These printed canvases by British artist Jon Burgerman are available directly from his website. They feature characters from his work on simple, single-coloured backgrounds. The roster of characters regularly changes, so once a character is sold out it may not be printed again. Each canvas is signed on the reverse.

329 x 483 mm (13 x 19 in)

Roderick Mills |
roderickmills.com

London-based Royal College of Art graduate Roderick Mills has developed an international profile, working for various clients in many areas of illustration. *Combination* is a limited-edition print that recycles his drawings from various projects to create a new artwork. This is an ongoing personal project in which he attempts to create new narratives out of old drawings. This is the first in a series documenting this process. It was produced in 2008 in an edition of 25.

'I think that the trend towards more self-initiated work and making products is really significant within the profession. The fact that websites are featuring shops to sell products enables the graphic designer to connect with an audience.'

Roderick Mills

Alexander Egger |
satellitesmistakenforstars.com

Graphic designer Alexander Egger regularly exhibits his work and creates and prints posters for the shows – usually in editions of 50 to 100. They are used to promote the shows and some are also sold. The size of his posters is usually A2, with the exception of his A1-size posters – shown here below and left – printed for the Synth Eastwood show, 'Worship', which took place in Dublin, Ireland, in late 2007. An additional run of seven posters was also later printed on demand at A2 size. The small text in the centre of the yellow *Worship* poster says '*Move along nothing to see here*'.

Below: *Now That Everything Is Over What Do You Want To Do Now* from Egger's 2008 show in Milano, Italy, and *A Pilotproject Exhibition* – front and back of poster shown – from his 2008 show in Graz, Austria.

Front | Back |

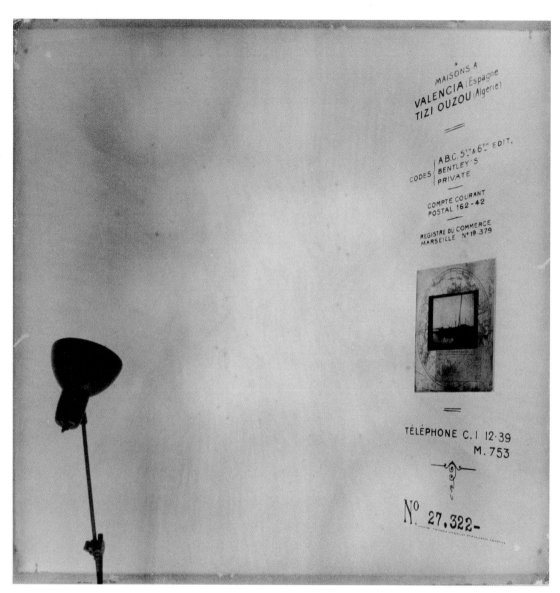

'When you design for yourself, you can push yourself to do things you may otherwise not even try to propose to clients... but when they see it, they want it for themselves because they see it works...'

Fabien Barral, Harmonie intérieure

Harmonie intérieure |
harmonie-interieure.com

Fabien Barral is a freelance photographer
and graphic designer based in St Bonnet
Près Orcival, Auvergne, France. In 2008 he
and his wife Frédérique set up Harmonie
intérieure – their new sideline, which
could easily become more than that. It's a
workshop where the pair offer their latest
range of home decoration pieces from a
wide selection of posters and mounted
pictures to typographic and illustrative
wall stickers – all bespoke – allowing
customers to choose individual sizes and
any of the 58 available sticker colours.

Jonathan Morris |
jonathanmorris.org.uk
sweetcreative.co.uk

The series *Microsea* by graphic designer Jonathan Morris – a surreal world of digital microscopic forms – won a prestigious competition run by Japanese design magazine *Shift*. In 2005, the project went on to form the basis of his first one-man show of digital art, 'Blend', at the CBAT Gallery in Cardiff. Creatively driven by his personal work, Jonathan's self-initiated projects provide him with the freedom to explore new techniques, which in turn fuel his commercial design studio, Sweet, based in Wales. Prints are available via his personal website.

'I prefer to have some separation between my commercial design work and personal creative development. I find that my work is answerable only to me and not a client or individual. This freedom allows a far more self-indulgent process and the outcome has a greater personal reward.'

Jonathan Morris

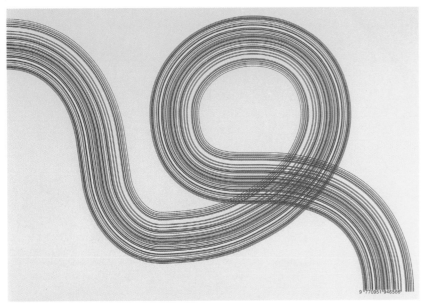

Julian Morey | Editions Eklektic
abc-xyz.co.uk
eklektic.co.uk

London-based graphic designer and typographer Julian Morey founded contemporary typeface foundry Club-21 in 1998 and established the publishing company Editions Eklektic in 2001 to showcase his more personal work in silkscreen prints and greetings cards. His *Space* silkscreen print – produced in red, black, fluorescent pink and fluorescent blue on 175 gsm paper – and *Rock and Roll* (which also featured on the front and back cover of the February 2002 edition of *Creative Review* magazine) are available as silkscreen prints in black and silver on 200 gsm paper. *Rock and Roll* greetings cards were also printed in black, gold and silver on 300 gsm paper.

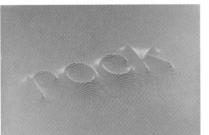  

| 508 x 762 mm (20 x 30 in)

| Cards: 182 x 122 mm (7¼ x 4¾ in)

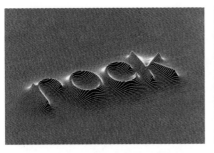

'Certain items, usually small and insignificant, excite me to the point where
I have to wear them and then document that process.'
Riitta Ikonen

Riitta Ikonen |
riittaikonen.com
reisesack.de

Originally from Finland, Riitta Ikonen is a London-based designer and artist. Her work is concerned with the performance of images through photography and costume design. Ikonen regularly collaborates with fellow Royal College of Art graduate Anja Schaffner – a German photographer – and between 2007 and 2008 the team created the project *Bird and Leaf – A Sentimental Yearning*. The series of photographic prints were produced in editions of 20 each, and are the first Ikonen made commercially available via her website and through exhibitions. So far she has not yet offered her fantastic one-off costumes for sale.

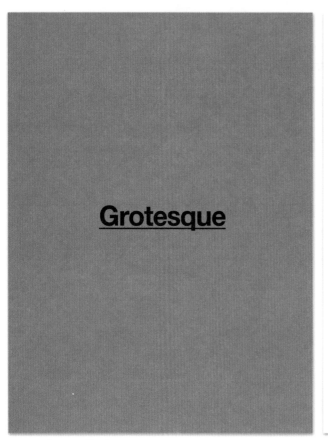

Grotesque

Interprétations typographiques saugrenues basées sur une récolte de caractères sans bâtons communément utilisé dans le domaine de la création graphique appliquée.

Poster composé en Helvetica Neue bold 75.

2008

~~Akzidenz Grotesk~~ Accident Grotesque

~~Helvetica Neue~~ Suisse Nouveau

~~Univers~~ Cosmos

~~Futura~~ Future ah !

~~Avenir~~ Postérieur

~~Frutiger~~ Fruité Guère

~~Gill Sans~~ Gilles Sent

peter&wendy

peter&wendy |
peter-wendy.com
xavierencinas.com

Front |

Back, 600 x 800 mm (23⅝ x 31½ in) |

Graphic designer Xavier Encinas and his Paris-based design studio peter&wendy created the double-sided *Grotesque* poster as one of their self-initiated pieces that later made it into production and is sold via their website. It was produced in an edition of 100 numbered copies, printed on 170 gsm offset paper in black and gold.

'We produce a variety of graphic projects including print, publishing, exhibition and event identity, corporate identity and anything else that gets us excited to get involved.'
Xavier Encinas, peter&wendy

CHK Design | Acme Fonts
chkdesign.com
acmefonts.net

German-born Christian Küsters runs his London-based multi-disciplinary design studio CHK Design and the type foundry and platform Acme Fonts that he established in 1999. Acme Fonts allows Küsters to showcase products that reflect his passion for experimental typography.

Left: *ArchiTypographic* from 2002 was a collaboration with architect–animators Gregory More and Nick McKenzie that explored the potential of moving typography beyond its two-dimensional surface. The poster's print run was 8,000.

Below: Küsters' *TypeFace* poster from 1999 was printed in an edition of 8,000. The back of the poster features a selection of his fonts.

| 545 x 820 mm (21½ x 32¼ in)

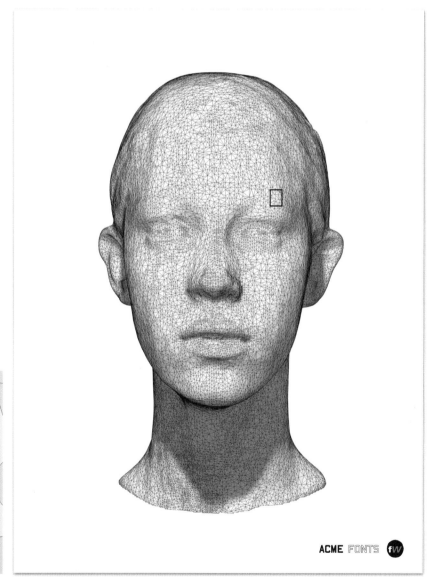

Back | Front, 410 x 545 mm (16⅛ x 21½ in) |

Hanna Werning, Spring Street Studio |

byhanna.com

Hanna Werning works as an independent designer across various disciplines, including communication and product design. She started working on her first wallpaper-posters in 2001 and set up Spring Street Studio in Stockholm, Sweden, in 2004.

Shown here are some of the pieces from her popular *AnimalFlowers* collection from 2005 and her *Tiles* poster from 2006. The wallpaper-poster pattern repeats from top to bottom and from left to right, and can be affixed to a clean, flat surface with wallpaper glue.

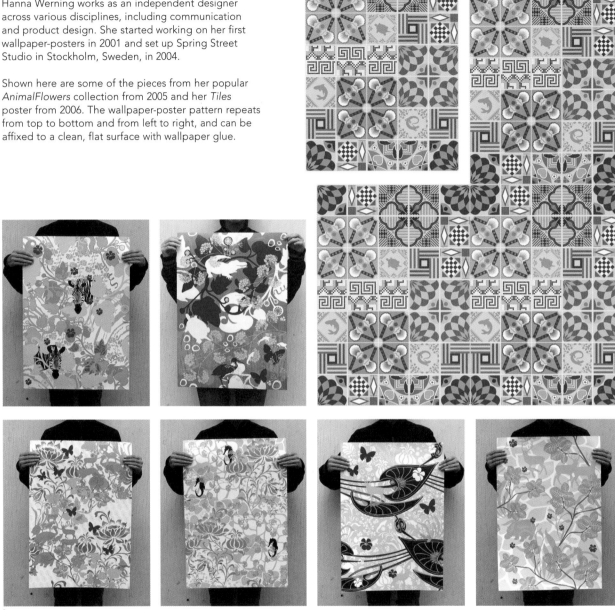

| 500 x 700 mm (19¾ x 27⅝ in)

'I started producing my wallpaper-posters while I was employed by Dan Eatock at Foundation 33. I got inspired by his way of working; doing great commercial work that enabled him to make and produce self-initiated work.'

Hanna Werning, Spring Street Studio

Maja Sten |
majasten.se

Stockholm-based freelancer Maja Sten studied at London's Royal College of Art and graduated in Communication Art and Design in 2002. Besides her commissioned work and her involvement in My Little Drama – a jewellery brand that she runs with Eva Schildt – Sten also creates self-initiated work such as her piece *Bedroom Drama*. It is a narrative wallpaper-poster inspired by the lamppost in the land of Narnia and was screen-printed in gold.

594 x 840 mm (23⅜ x 33⅛ in) per sheet

Kapitza | Kapitza Shop
kapitza.com

London-based Kapitza is an independent design company run by sisters Nicole and Petra Kapitza who share a passion for everyday life, minimalism, patterns and colour. The sisters have been developing an extensive series of unique picture-fonts and illustrations that lie somewhere between image resource and art project. Illustrations like *Herbarium* from 2008 (left) are made available in their online shop as either vector graphics or signed digital prints.

594 x 840 mm (23⅜ x 33⅛ in)

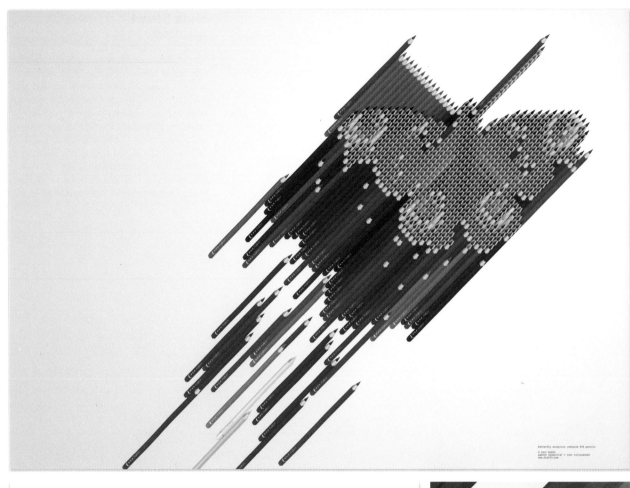

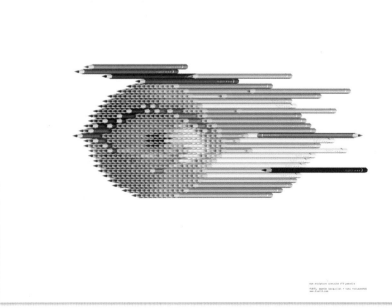

Detail ▶

'It is very important for us to maintain a healthy balance between commissioned and self-initiated projects – it keeps us and our clients happy.'

Agathe Jacquillat and Tomi Vollauschek, FL@33

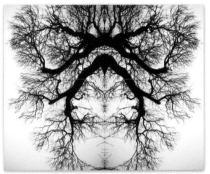

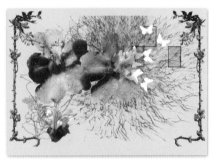

FL@33 | Stereohype
flat33.com
stereohype.com

FL@33 founders Agathe Jacquillat and Tomi Vollauschek regularly create and produce posters and prints that they make available via exhibitions and their sister-company stereohype.com.

Opposite page: 'Pencil Sculpture' illustration series: A1-size *Butterfly Sculpture* contains 818 pencils, and A2-size *Eye Sculpture* contains 470 pencils. Prints were first produced digitally in 2002 for Laurence King's *GB: Graphic Britain* book launch exhibition at Magma, London. Pencils are life-size on the prints. Both self-initiated pieces led to a commission for a front and back cover illustration of *Creative Review* magazine's feature article '40 Years of D&AD', November 2002.

Left, top and second from top: *Deer* and *Hibernation* from 2004 were first published as part of a series of commissioned FL@33 artworks in the 'Mirror' issue of Barcelona-based magazine *The Creator Studio*. The 'Tree' series is inspired by the ten secret plates of Hermann Rorschach and plays with the concepts of folding and symmetry. Digital prints on matt photographic paper, 406 x 508 mm (16 x 20 in).

Left, middle: Digital A1-size print, mixed-media illustration *Spring #1*, from 2003.

Left, second from bottom: *Shadows, passers-by seen from Eiffel Tower* is an artwork from 2003. Digital print on matt photographic paper, 406 x 508 mm (16 x 20 in).

Left, bottom: A2-size *Dalai Lama Speech*, FL@33's contribution to the poster exhibition 'Public Address System', 2004. Two-colour offset-printed on 70 gsm, numbered, limited edition of 300 (sold out).

Above: *Street Typeface 33* from 2003 is based on aerial photography by Fenwick Helicopters, Paris. Digital print on matt photographic paper, 406 x 508 mm (16 x 20 in).

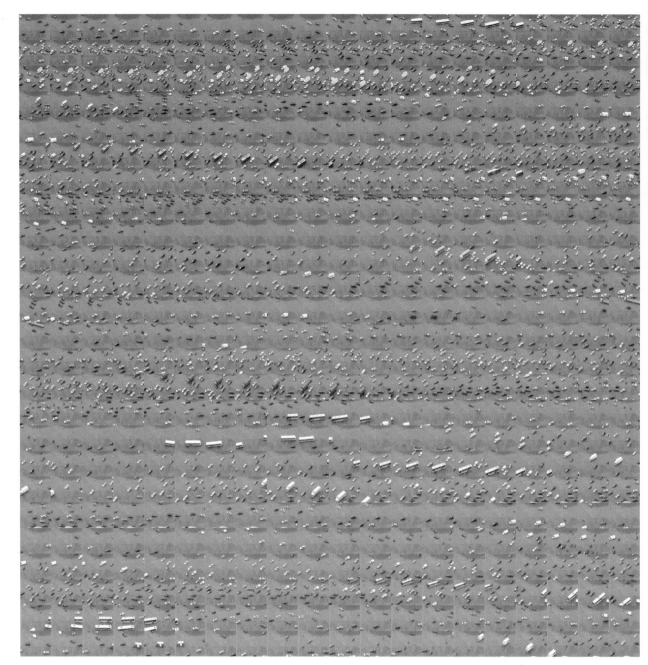

Detail **I**

'We always try to find the most appropriate concept, visual language and medium for all our projects – commissioned or self-initiated – and ideally the final work speaks for itself.'
Agathe Jacquillat and Tomi Vollauschek, FL@33

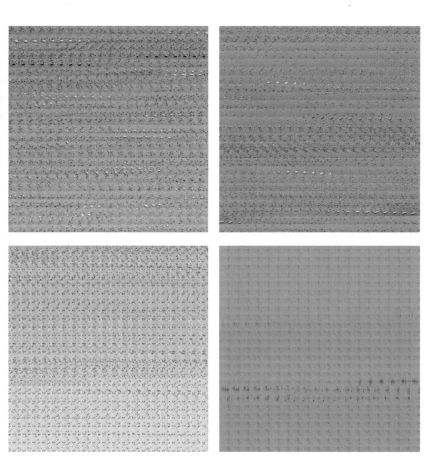

FL@33 | Stereohype
flat33.com
stereohype.com

Left and opposite page: *8 min 20 sec* by London-based FL@33 is a series of photographic prints. The concept is based on capturing a city (in this case Paris) in video sequences of 8 minutes and 20 seconds (= 500 seconds). Each video was then reduced to one frame per second. The resulting prints are based on the individual collections of 500 frames and are arranged into square compositions. The sequences were created between 2002 and 2005 and were first exhibited – accompanied by video animations for plasma screens – in 2004 during a solo exhibition in Paris entitled '8 min 20 sec'. Numbered and signed prints are available at stereohype.com in a limited edition of 33 each and come in two sizes: 400 x 400 mm (15¾ x15¾ in) or 900 x 900 mm (35⅜ x 35⅜ in). Original video sequences were taken by FL@33 from the top of the Arc de Triomphe in Paris and from level two of the Eiffel Tower.

Below: More experiments included *8 min 20 sec – Little Venice, London* and *20 sec – Millennium Bridge, London – a boat trip on the River Thames.*

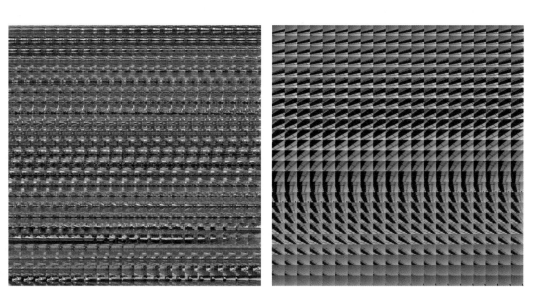

Fonts and Typographic 3D Products |

This chapter is real eye-candy for typophiles.
Selected examples give a good overview of current
typographic activities that result in a distinctive
product – be it a font, lenticular print, house number,
typographic hand-rail, kite in the shape of a letter, a
game or a temporary signage system.

Box containing 64 cubes

'*I am interested in mediating the gap between design and the public and exploring design's ability to facilitate and benefit social change.*'
Chris Clarke

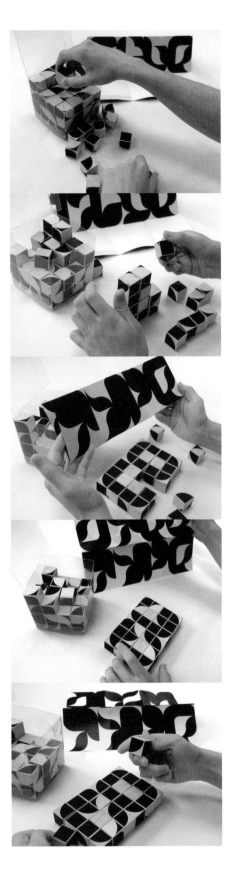

Chris Clarke |
chris-clarke.co.uk

Chris Clarke is a recent Graphic Design graduate from the University of the West of England. Adopting the assertion 'In order to change things, we must first attain a decent understanding of them' he is interested in bridging the gap between design and the public, and exploring design's ability to facilitate and benefit social change. His *Typecube – Modular Typeface Design* is a design tool used to facilitate the modular construction of letterforms. *Typecube's* six faces each bear a unique formal component which provides the basis of two-dimensional and three-dimensional typographic systems, encouraging flexibility within uniform structure. By varying the number of typecubes, typographic solutions vary in complexity, and are capable of infinite rearrangement.

Medium |
mediumism.com

Medium is a creative studio based in Stockholm, which produces projects related to public space, architecture and visual culture. Projects by Medium often focus on the context of our everyday lives; the commonplace things that often go unnoticed. Medium is run by Jake Ford, Martin Frostner and Lisa Olausson. In 2007 they invited ten typographers and graphic designers from different backgrounds and countries, and of different ages, to design a house number. House numbers are everywhere but are seldom considered as designed objects. Each designer was asked to produce a single numeral between one and nine – and Medium drew the short straw with zero. As the house numbers then go into double figures, the designers are paired together in different combinations.

1 – James Goggin
2 – Paul Elliman
3 – Julian Morey
4 – Sara De Bondt
5 – Margaret Calvert
6 – Anthony Burrill
7 – Anisa Suthayalai
8 – Norm
9 – Alan Kitching
0 – Medium

'Medium is a vehicle for us to produce self-initiated projects, and some of those end up as objects. Producing a product is a very tangible way to engage the general public.'
Jake Ford, Martin Frostner and Lisa Olausson, Medium

Andrew Byrom |
andrewbyrom.com

Andrew Byrom was born in Liverpool, UK. After
graduating in 1997 he opened his own studio in
London. Byrom moved to America in 2000 and now
lives in Los Angeles. He now divides his time between
teaching, designing for various clients and working
on his own self-initiated three-dimensional typefaces.
Grab-Me from 2006 is a full alphabet set made from
1.5 diameter stainless-steel tubing with a 180 grit
brushed finish. These finished typographic hand-rails
are intended for use in swimming pools or bathrooms.
They can be used indoors or outside, so they can also
be used as building signage. *Grab-Me* was honoured
with a Type Directors Award (TDC, New York) in 2007.

'I used to see myself as a type designer, but my ultimate goal now is to make and sell typographic objects and products.'
Andrew Byrom

Andrew Byrom |
andrewbyrom.com

Opposite page, top: These low-relief, three-dimensional, ultra-thin, folded aluminium numbers from 2008 are intended for use on houses and offices. They are manufactured in anodized, weatherproof aluminium.

Opposite page, bottom: Byrom's experimental *Letter-Box-Kite* design from 2008 is a series of 26 typographic kites made from thin nylon fabric and fibreglass poles.

This page: *Byrom TSS* from 2007 is a 'pop-up' temporary signage system. Each letter is fabricated from waterproof nylon wrapped around a fibreglass pole frame, similar to the construction of a modern dome tent. An elastic cord running inside the hollow poles allows the design to collapse into a small bag for storage. The design is intended for temporary use in shops, galleries, conferences and so on.

Kapitza | Kapitza Shop
kapitza.com

Kapitza is an independent, London-based design company set up by sisters Nicole and Petra Kapitza. In 2006 they opened up the online Kapitza Shop, realizing that they stood to glean greater profit and to exercise more creative freedom if they sold their own picture fonts directly to the public, rather than selling them through other foundries. The sisters share a passion for everyday life, minimalism, pattern and colour.

Architekt, 2006, picture font, OpenType

Dalston, 2007, people silhouette font, OpenType

'We only do commissioned work now if we are really interested in the project. We feel that our time is best spent doing our self-initiated projects and working with complete creative freedom.'
Nicole and Petra Kapitza

Twirl, 2008, illustration, 300dpi TIFF files with transparent background ▎

▎ *We Love Nature*, 2007, flower illustration, vector

Herbarium, 2008, flower illustration, vector ▎

▎ *Generation Z*, 2007, kids' portrait illustrations, vector

Matt Burvill, HouseOfBurvo |
houseofburvo.co.uk

HouseOfBurvo is the home for all of graphic designer Matt Burvill's sidelines. It functions as portfolio, font foundry and freelance portal. HouseOfBurvo will be focusing its energies on the font foundry more and more as time goes on, as this has always been the founder's true love.

Shown here are his fonts Geometric Hairline Serif (this page) and on the opposite page (left to right from top): Architect, Babys Definite Hit, Optical, Killer, Pump and Bürvo Konstrukteur – his most comprehensive font family to date. They consist of seven weights from Extra Light to Extra Black.

The compositions were created especially for this book.

'I started with the font shop, which was born of a feeling that I shouldn't be keeping these things to myself and that other people could enjoy them.'

Matt Burvill, HouseOfBurvo

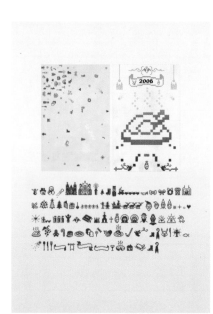

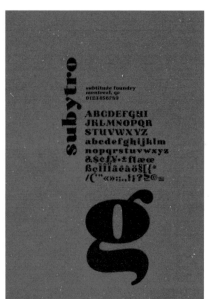

'We have complete freedom at our sideline department, Subtitude, which allows us to experiment with typography, illustrations and non-commissioned graphics.'
Valérie Desrochers and Sébastien Théraulaz, Subcommunication/Subtitude

Subcommunication | Subtitude
subcommunication.com
subtitude.com

Canadian graphic designer Valérie
Desrochers and Switzerland-born Sébastien
Théraulaz run Montréal-based design
studio Subcommunication. They split their
time between commissioned work and
self-initiated projects, such as passionately
designing fonts that they release via their
sideline department Subtitude.

Opposite page, left to right from top:
The pair's fonts *Suboel* from 2005, *Subikto
One* from 2006 and *Subikto Two* from
2007, Desrochers' *Subytro* and *Subelair*
from 2006 and *Subroyal*, which they
developed in collaboration with Frédéric
Fivaz from Switzerland, a former member
of Sub.

Left: The font *Subinter* from 2003.

CHK Design | Acme Fonts
chkdesign.com
acmefonts.net

London-based Christian Küsters designed
AF Metropolis (above and opposite page,
bottom) at his multi-disciplinary design
studio CHK Design and digital type
foundry, Acme Fonts. It was an experiment
to explore a three-dimensional space on
the two-dimensional surface of a page
or screen. Designed by Küsters in
collaboration with Paul Beavis, who did
the three-dimensional modelling, the
visuals were featured on the front and
back cover of *Creative Review* magazine,
July 2002.

Opposite page, top: Küsters font set
AF Zip Code includes the weights light,
regular, medium and bold.

*'The motivation behind Acme Fonts stems from a great interest in typeface experimentation.
Clients do not always ask for this kind of work, consequently leading me to
become my own client to satisfy my creative curiosity.'*
Christian Küsters, CHK Design/Acme Fonts

ABCDEFGHIJKLM
OPQRSTUVWXYZ
abcdefghijklm
nopqrstuvwxyz
1234567890

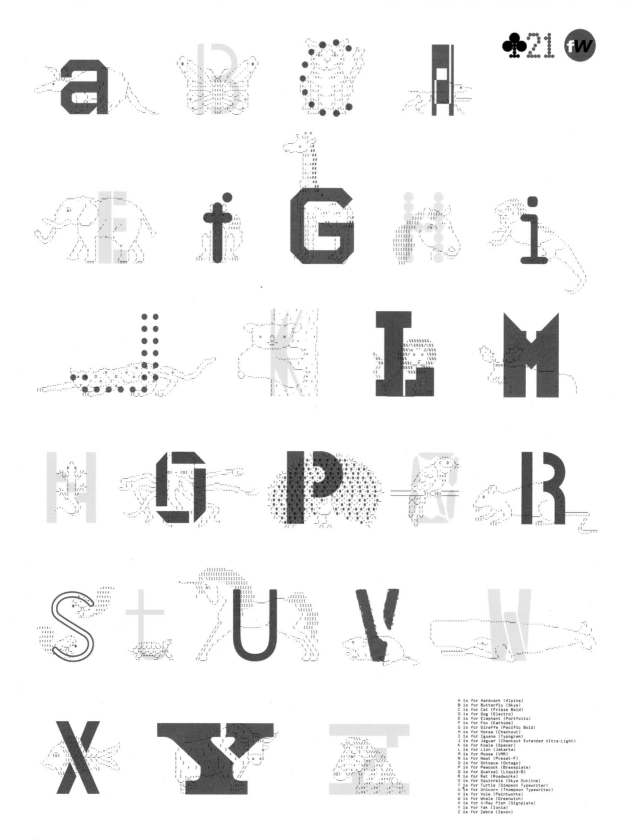

'We're presently at a time where designers use sidelines as part of their marketing mix. Instead of producing a catalogue of your work to promote yourself you might make a product based around a unique concept.'

Julian Morey

```
A is for Aardvark (Alpine)
B is for Butterfly (Skye)
C is for Cat (Frieze Bold)
D is for Dog (Electro)
E is for Elephant (Portfolio)
F is for Fox (Kathode)
G is for Giraffe (Pacific Bold)
H is for Horse (Checkout)
I is for Iguana (Typogram)
J is for Jaguar (Checkout Extended Ultra-Light)
K is for Koala (Spacer)
L is for Lion (Jakarta)
M is for Moose (VMR)
N is for Newt (Preset-F)
O is for Octopus (Octago)
P is for Peacock (Brassplate)
Q is for Quetzal (Liquid-B)
R is for Rat (Roadworks)
S is for Squirrels (Skye Outline)
T is for Turtle (Simpson Typewriter)
U is for Unicorn (Thompson Typewriter)
V is for Vole (Paintworks)
W is for Whale (Greenwich)
X is for X-Ray Fish (Signplate)
Y is for Yak (Ionia)
Z is for Zebra (Zexon)
```

| Detail from Morey's poster

Julian Morey | Club-21
abc-xyz.co.uk
eklektic.co.uk

Opposite page: Julian Morey's
contemporary typeface foundry Club-21
was founded in 1998. He created this
ASCII-art poster to promote his collection.
The poster featured ASCII illustrations by
Joan Stark.

Atelier télescopique | Ainsi Font
ateliertelescopique.com
ainsifont.com

One of the many sideline activities of
Atelier télescopique (based in Lille, France)
is their digital typeface foundry Ainsi Font,
and their creations are available online.
Above is a poster promoting the release
of their font family *Zofage CPS*, which
comes in six weights: light, regular, bold,
heavy, outline and stencil.

*'Visionary ideas, from Da Vinci's notion of a helicopter to
Edison's lightbulb, were hardly ever the result of a commission.
Inventions and innovations occur freely and independently from pragmatic constraints.
Their use and commercial exploitation may or may not happen at a later stage.'*
Matthias Hillner, Studio for Virtual Typography

Studio for Virtual Typography |
virtualtypography.com

Matthias Hillner from Germany studied at the Royal College of Art in London. He obtained a Masters degree in 2001 and an MPhil from the RCA a few years later. He set up his Studio for Virtual Typography in London in 2005 and provides services in the field of visual communication and explores the potential of typographic expression in the context of fine art.

Horizons is a series of large-format prints that reveal philosophical reflections on contemporary urban surroundings and on the pace of life they induce. Depending on the viewing angle, the messages may be concealed. The viewer is forced to move around the prints to unveil their typographic messages. The lenticular prints are available in six colours: orange, cyan, turquoise, sepia, red and blue, in editions of five per colour. All prints are available in all six colours.

From left to right:
Gravity, sepia, 2007, Willis Building reflecting details of Lloyds Building, London, UK;
Desire, red, 2007, Hypobank Building, Munich, Germany;
Open Sky, turquoise, 2007, La Grande Arche, La Défense, France;
Open Sky, orange, 2006, La Grande Arche, La Défense, France;
Mind Frame, cyan, 2007, No. 1 London Bridge, London, UK.
The prints feature Hillner's registered typeface *Cubico Stencil*.

| 1,220 x 800 mm (48 x 31½ in)

Clothing |

The T-shirt is probably one of the most popular articles on which artists and designers like to print their artworks for others to buy and wear. This section is really only a snapshot of the clothing products available. We did, however, unearth some amazing highlights, including fantastic night and day T-shirts featuring alternative night-glow motifs. There is also the *Lowercase t-shirt* and some classic garments by pioneering US-based label Green Lady set up by HunterGatherer's Todd St. John and designer Gary Benzel.

'We felt the need to create our own products to express ourselves fully and we do actually have even more activities including teaching, drawing, designing, tattooing ...'
Patch, Happypets

Happypets | Happypets Products
happypets.ch

These T-shirts, by Lausanne-based Happypets, are called *Slice for rent* (opposite page), *Yo!*, *Mansion*, *Blind stomach*, *No bread just meat* (this page, left to right from top). All were screen-printed in 2005 in limited editions of 25.

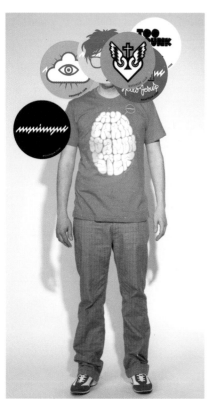

'Working on internal projects and developing our own products in addition to working for our clients was simply the logical outcome.'
Atelier télescopique, Wassingue

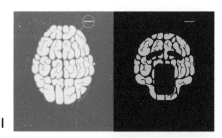

My brain is a monster |

Sick boy |

Rain flips our smile |

De Tijger |

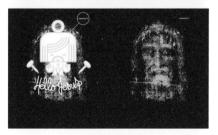

Hello Jesus |

Love Song |

Atelier télescopique | Wassingue
ateliertelescopique.com
wassingue.com

Stéphane Meurice, Sébastien Delobel, Xavier Meurice, Guillaume Berry and Baptiste Servais make up Lille-based design studio Atelier télescopique. Wassingue – Floor Clothes Design – is one of the team's side projects. *Wassingue* means 'floor cloth' in northern French patois and comes from the English word 'washing'. They created this brand in 2003 and launched their first T-shirt collection for the general public in early 2008.

The photographs show the different models from their 'Collection 01'. The distinctive feature of this collection is that a T-shirt looks different in daylight than it does at night, due to an additional layer of night-glow ink. As a result, each T-shirt motif has two facets.

Intercity |
intercitydesign.com

Intercity is a London-based graphic
design studio, formed in 2004 by Nick
Foot, Nathan Gale and Tu Hoang. These
beautifully screen-printed T-shirts first
appeared in the book *300% Cotton* by
Helen Walters. To create the wrap-around
print design, four separate screens were
used for the black *Cityscape* T-shirt and
two separate screens for the yellow one.

*'Some of our T-shirt and badge designs were originally created from
client-commissioned projects that never happened, but since making them for
ourselves we have had new client commissions based on this personal work.'*

Nathan Gale, Intercity

Peepshow | Peepshop
peepshow.org.uk
peepshop.org.uk

The silkscreen-printed T-shirt *Honk for Peace* by Luke Best was produced in 2008 in an edition of just 25. It is one of many fantastic T-shirts that the Peepshow collective regularly creates and produces for their own product sideline.

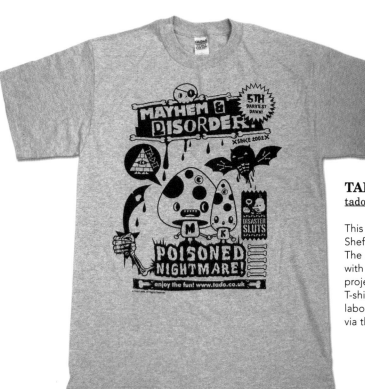

TADO |
tado.co.uk

This screen-printed T-shirt was created by Sheffield-based Mike and Katie of TADO. The pair always keep themselves busy with personal and collaborative sideline projects and their *Mayhem & Disorder* T-shirt is just one of many fruits of their labours that regularly become available via their website.

'The ability to develop self-motivated projects heavily influences my design process, and my curiosity as a designer.'
Chris Clarke

Chris Clarke |
chris-clarke.co.uk

London-based graphic designer Chris Clarke collaborated with Holly Lloyd in 2008 to create this typographic interpretation of a traditional T-shirt using the form of a lowercase letter 't'. The *Lowercase t-shirt* is both unisex and adaptable.

HunterGatherer | Green Lady
huntergatherer.net
greenlady.com

Todd St. John is an artist, designer and film-maker living in New York City. St. John produces both commercial and experimental work through HunterGatherer, the studio/workshop that he founded in 2000. St. John also co-founded the influential graphic T-shirt label Green Lady with Gary Benzel. *Nylon Magazine* described Green Lady as 'to the designer T-shirt world what Run-DMC is to hip hop'.

These assorted T-shirts and hoodies were silkscreen-printed and released between 1999 and 2003.

'I've never thought about client-driven work and product-driven work as separate things, so I've always done both. They both have their audiences, and a big part of my work has always been about talking to people in non-rarefied settings.'

Todd St. John, HunterGatherer

Nous Vous |
nousvous.eu

Nous Vous are predominately a graphic design, art direction and illustration studio, working both as individuals and as a team on a wide range of projects.

The witty *Siamese Beards* T-shirts were screen-printed as a small edition of eight and we can reveal here that there may be future editions. The other two T-shirts are one-off vinyl designs. All T-shirts were made by Nicolas Burrows in 2008.

'Seeing a Tottenham Hotspur fan wearing one of my Tottenham White Hart Lane Stadium Footprint T-shirts, with the actual stadium in the background, was a good moment!'

Jeff Knowles

| The Old Wembley Stadium

| The New Wembley Stadium

Jeff Knowles |

mosjef.com
shotdeadinthehead.com

British graphic designer Jeff Knowles joined Research Studios, London, in 1998. His self-initiated 'Football Club Stadium Footprint' T-shirts, created in his spare time, feature the aerial footprints of football stadiums and their surrounding roads. Neither the name of the football club nor the name of the stadium is featured on the T-shirt, so only a true fan of the club will recognize the ground.

Opposite page, left to right, top to bottom:

01 – Liverpool Football Club, Anfield
02 – Fulham Football Club, Craven Cottage
03 – Middlesbrough Football Club, Riverside Stadium
04 – Reading Football Club, Madejski Stadium
05 – Chelsea Football Club, Stamford Bridge
06 – Manchester City Football Club, City Of Manchester Stadium
07 – Aston Villa Football Club, Villa Park
08 – Manchester United Football Club, Old Trafford
09 – West Ham United Football Club, Boleyn
10 – Blackburn Rovers Football Club, Ewood Park
11 – Charlton Athletic Football Club, The Valley
12 – Bolton Wanders Football Club, Reebok Stadium
13 – Wigan Athletic Football Club, JJb Stadium
14 – Tottenham Hotspur Football Club, White Hart Lane
15 – Watford Football Club, Vicarage Road
16 – Newcastle United Football Club, St James' Park
17 – Arsenal Football Club, Emirates Stadium
18 – Portsmouth Football Club, Fratton Park
19 – Sheffield United Football Club, Bramall Lane
20 – Birmingham City Football Club, St Andrews

'I think diversification is very important for a designer, as it not only increases the skillset that you can offer clients, it also helps educate you in the commercial world, which is an asset when dealing with clients. For me, it also keeps me interested and challenged creatively.'

Jeremy Andrew, Jeremyville

Jeremyville |
jeremyville.com

Jeremy Andrew owns and runs the project-based studio called Jeremyville. He produces animation, design, art, ad campaigns and artist-based collaborative projects for various international clients. His self-initiated activities include frequent releases of limited-edition T-shirts that are available via his website.

Supersentido |

supersentido.cl

Below: Santiago-based designer and illustrator Supersentido designed and screen-printed these T-shirts, which feature typical and vernacular graphics from Chile. They were produced between 2005 and 2006 in limited editions of 100 each.

Add Fuel To The Fire | Ignited

addfueltothefire.com
addfueltothefire.com/shop
ignitedclothing.com

Opposite page, top: Ignited clothing is Diogo Machado's playground brand with exclusive artwork from his studio, Add Fuel To The Fire, based in Portugal. Ignited was launched in 2007 and these are some of the T-shirts from his first collection.

Paulo Arraiano | Palm

pauloarraiano.com
palmshirts.com

Opposite page, bottom: Paulo Arraiano, aka Yup, co-founded Palm in Portugal together with Leonor Morais. Palm is a brand intended to serve as a forum for experimentation in Portuguese design, illustration and street art, as well as for international collaborations. Arraiano's T-shirts *Lovespread*, *Suparunin* and *Powawa* were screen-printed in 2008.

'It's such a great feeling to see somebody wearing your design!'
Supersentido

'The motivation was to create cool designs that other people (and us) could wear.'
Danny Geerlof/DTM INC, Frogbite

DTM INC | Frogbite
frogbite.nl

Opposite page: Danny Geerlof, aka DTM
INC ('Dan The Man Incorporated'), is an
employed graphic designer who launched
Dutch online T-shirt shop frogbite.nl in
2005 together with two of his friends.

123Klan | Bandit-1$m
123klan.com
123klan.bigcartel.com

Above: Montréal-based graffiti artists
Scien and Klor, aka 123Klan, created these
self-initiated T-shirt motifs in 2008 for their
sideline 'Bandit-1$m'.

FL@33 | Stereohype

flat33.com
stereohype.com
bzzzpeek.com

In 2004, London-based design studio FL@33 launched their sister company Stereohype, an online graphic art and fashion boutique offering limited editions and rare – and most importantly fresh, innovative and inspirational – products. Stereohype.com is a platform for designers and artists from around the world. Regular competitions give emerging and established artists, illustrators and designers the chance to promote their talent and to get their artwork produced and featured.

Here are a few of the FL@33-designed garments that have been screen-printed for Stereohype.

Above: *Butterflies in my Stomach*, 2004.

Right: *Stereohype Squirrel* short-sleeved shirt from 2005.

Opposite page: *Paris* and *New York* were two of the city motifs to be produced as part of the 'Coin-operated Telescope' series from 2004.

'Initially we were considering launching an official FL@33-only shop for our self-published products but came to the conclusion that it would be more enjoyable for us (and our customers) to create a platform for other designers and artists, too.'

Agathe Jacquillat and Tomi Vollauschek, FL@33

'Our self-initiated project bzzzpeek.com was always supposed to be a non-profit project.
We hesitated for a long time before we introduced our support T-shirts to help finance the
out-of-control server costs generated by up to 15,000 unique visitors per day.'
Agathe Jacquillat and Tomi Vollauschek, FL@33

quack quack

FL@33 | Stereohype
flat33.com
stereohype.com
bzzzpeek.com

T-shirts for the whole family, produced to
support the popular sound collection of
recorded onomatopoeia from around
the world, bzzzpeek.com, that FL@33
launched in 2002. The FL@33-designed
T-shirts are screen-printed on organic
cotton and are available via the studio's
online boutique, stereohype.com.

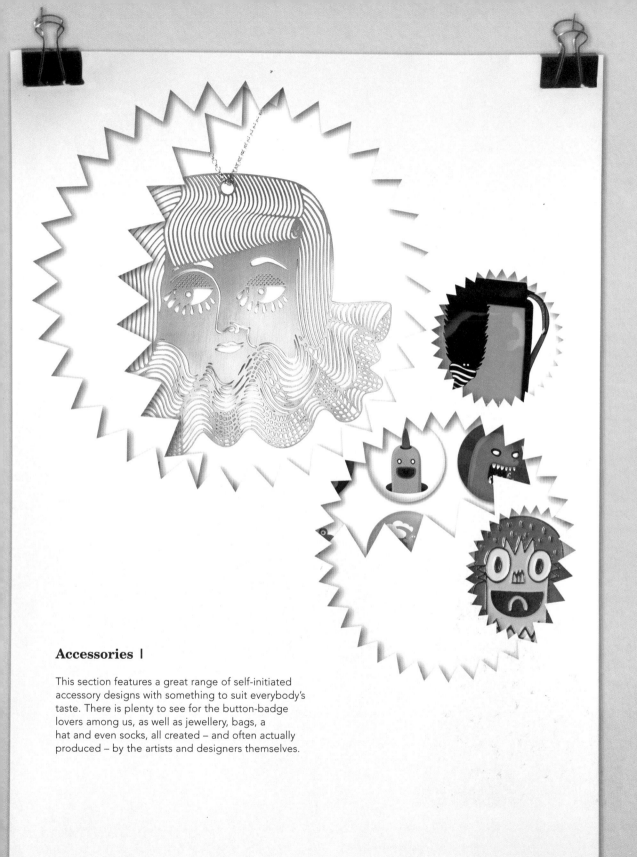

Accessories |

This section features a great range of self-initiated
accessory designs with something to suit everybody's
taste. There is plenty to see for the button-badge
lovers among us, as well as jewellery, bags, a
hat and even socks, all created – and often actually
produced – by the artists and designers themselves.

Gareth Holt and William Smith | FlatHat

assemblylondon.com
smithandwightman.com

Gareth Holt graduated from the Royal College of Art in 2004, and has since set up his own multi-disciplinary design studio The-Projects and, together with fellow RCA graduate Ben Branagan, he runs London-based Assembly. Holt shares a studio space with product designer William Smith from Smith&Wightman and the two collaborated to develop the *FlatHat* – a hybrid of a cap, beanie hat and bespoke dress hat.

The *FlatHat* is a unisex design from 2008, which has all the practical applications of a sports hat combined with a street aesthetic. The design of the *FlatHat* and its lattice cuts means that it can be folded, stuffed or rolled within a pocket when not being worn, without being crushed or damaging the structure. It is made of 2.5 mm high-grade 100 per cent natural wool felt and is available in a variety of colours. A summer version of 1.5 mm high-grade wool felt is also available and a rubber cork version is in production.

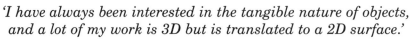

'I have always been interested in the tangible nature of objects, and a lot of my work is 3D but is translated to a 2D surface.'

Gareth Holt, Assembly

DGPH |
dgph.com.ar
molestown.com

Among the most recent DGPH products are their *Mole* socks. The colourways include (from right to left) a regular version (green), Japan LA colourway (pink), the Funkrush colourway (black) and MyPlasticHeart special edition (grey). The socks were released during the 2008 DGPH exhibition 'Criaturas Nocturnas' (night creatures) in Buenos Aires, Argentina.

'The positive feedback we got for our sideline projects, such as our button-badge design initiative B.I.O. (by invitation only) series, encouraged us to conceive our own book projects like the one you are holding in your hands at the moment.'

Agathe Jacquillat and Tomi Vollauschek, FL@33

FL@33 | Stereohype

flat33.com
stereohype.com

Once or twice a year FL@33 invites emerging and established designers, illustrators and artists from around the world to contribute designs for their growing button-badge collection. Individual series are called B.I.O. (by invitation only), followed by the edition number, and so far the collection includes over 400 individual designs by B.I.O. contributors and winners of the annual badge design competition (open to the public) organized by Stereohype. Badges are sold separately or in sets and are given away as free surprise goodies with purchased Stereohype T-shirts. Shown here are contributions by FL@33 and Stereohype founders Agathe Jacquillat and Tomi Vollauschek – who, as hosts, always take part themselves – from B.I.O. series 1–7, created between 2004 and 2008.

Quite a few of the artists who have already created mobile mini-canvases for the Stereohype button-badge collection also contributed to this very book, and include Jon Burgerman, Brighten the Corners, Intercity, Anthony Burrill, Tom Gauld, Zeptonn, Andy Smith, Supersentido, Artiva, Alexander Egger, Birgit Simons, Happypets, Peepshow, Jeffrey Bowman, Jonathan Morris, Judith Egger, Julian Morey, Lunartik JOnes, Roderick Mills, Matthias Hillner, Musa, Riitta Ikonen, Medium, Rinzen, Twopoints.Net and 123Klan.

Zeptonn |
zeptonn.nl

Examples of some of the button
badges frequently released by Dutch
freelance illustrator Jan Willem Wennekes,
aka Zeptonn.

'If you only ever do client work, this is what potential clients will see and hence that is what they will commission you for. However, if you also show artwork that you feel good about, even though you consider it unusable for commercial projects, you never know what might happen.'
Jan Willem Wennekes, Zeptonn

Intercity |
intercitydesign.com

Badge/Button/Pin badge packs were created in conjunction with Gavin Lucas – author of the Intercity-designed book *Badge/Button/Pin* published by Laurence King Publishing in 2007. Packs of badges are either designed by Intercity or by a collaborating image-maker. The first three packs were released in editions of 40 each.

Emmi Salonen |
emmi.co.uk

Emmi Salonen – originally from Finland –
has run London-based design studio Emmi
since 2005. She divides her time between
commissioned work, working as a sessional
tutor at Ravensbourne and New Bucks
Universities and self-initiated projects
such as her popular button badges.

*'I suppose as a graphic designer I am commissioned to convey someone else's message,
by profession. And sometimes I've just got things to say myself.'*

Emmi Salonen, Emmi

Jon Burgerman |
jonburgerman.com

These button and metal badges feature Jon Burgerman's characters. The metal badges are exclusive either to a certain product or, like the famous Blue Peter badge, can only be attained for special achievements. They are given directly by the artist to the recipient. Sometimes they are sent along with orders from his online shop to regular customers as a small thank you for their support.

Greig Anderson | Effektive

effektivedesign.co.uk
effektiveblog.com

Graphic designer Greig Anderson graduated in 2004 with a degree in Applied Graphics and then worked at multi-disciplinary agency Curious, in Glasgow. Anderson also produces various freelance work for clients and self-initiated projects including button badges, posters and T-shirt designs under the name of Effektive, which he set up in 2007. Anderson moved to Sydney in summer 2008 where he works at design studio There.

Anderson has produced 12 sets of six 25 mm (1in) button badges from the 12 mainstream cassette types he remembers from his childhood. The badges are created as circular crops of the actual cassette artwork. These are attached to a printed cassette back board and sealed in a classic cassette box with a custom inlay card giving a brief history of the cassette format.

Tape images supplied courtesy of Tapedeck, www.tapedeck.org.

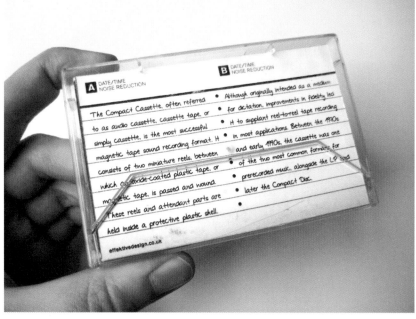

'The button badges came around after I received a button press as a present and I started to enjoy the challenge of working within a 25 mm (1in) diameter canvas.'

Greig Anderson, Effektive

'brew'

'alpaca'

Kate Sutton |
katesutton.co.uk
katesutton.etsy.com

Here are a few of the badge sets that illustrator Kate Sutton has released over the years, alongside her plush creatures (see pages 70–71). Her work has been featured in books and magazines, on buses, T-shirts, plasters and bags, and she has even done a few tattoo commissions.

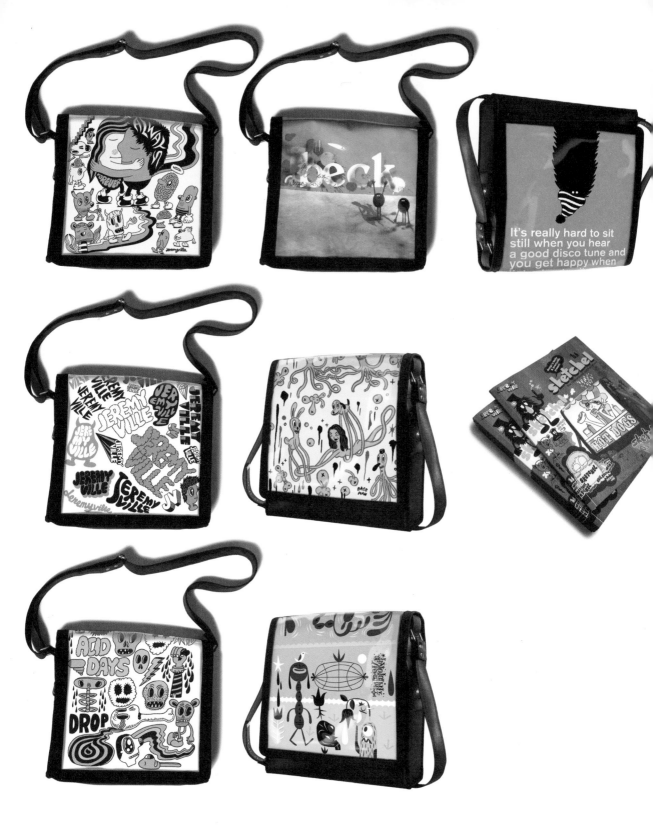

It's really hard to sit
still when you hear
a good disco tune and
you get happy when

'Since I first started my studio, and when I screen-printed my first T-shirts,
I was happily also doing work for clients, so the two strands have always gone hand in hand.
In fact, I would not be comfortable only doing one or the other; I feel fulfilled by both areas.'

Jeremy Andrew, Jeremyville

Jeremyville |
jeremyville.com

Opposite page: Jeremyville initiated the popular *Sketchel* custom art satchel project in collaboration with around 500 international artists. The first three bags, shown here in the far left-hand column, are by Jeremyville himself. Jeremyville's *Acid Days Sketchel*, *Forever and Always Sketchel* and *Text Sketchel* were all screen-printed in 2008. The sketchels shown in the centre column are the collaborative bag by musician Beck and illustrator Geneviève Gauckler, and designs by Gary Baseman and Tim Biskup. The backward sketchel on the right is another by Paris-based Geneviève Gauckler. Sketchels are usually produced in non-limited editions – the only exception being the collaborative Beck/Gauckler one, which was produced in 2007 in a limited edition of 200.

The *Sketchel* book features about 160 sketchel designs and was published in 2005 to coincide with the launch of the sketchel project at Semi Permanent design conference hosted by Design is Kinky.

Left: Button badges from 2007.

*'Working with my hands adds another dimension to creativity,
and making products is a great way to involve others in my way of designing and thinking.'*
Birgit Simons, BBags

Birgit Simons | BBags
birgitsimons.de

Frankfurt-based graphic designer Birgit Simons lived in Japan for over three years from 2005. The density of inspiration and the new exotic environment had a deep impact on her design. In 2007 she relaunched her sideline BBags – bags and accessories made from vintage materials – this time using japanese *obi*, the beautiful and colourful sash that ties the kimono.

The magic fusion of Japanese and western culture revives traditional materials and patterns for modern life – a piece of Japan and a product that tells its own story, timeless and fashionable at the same time. All items are made from high-quality vintage silk brocade. Due to the fact that the fabric is limited and the products handmade, each BBag is unique.

Maja Sten and Eva Schildt |
My Little Drama

mylittledrama.com
majasten.se
evaschildt.se

Product designer Eva Schildt and illustrator Maja Sten launched Stockholm-based My Little Drama in 2008, where they showcase and sell their collaborative jewellery. The two have known each other since 1978, when they used to draw sad puppies at kindergarten.

The collection consists of a number of motifs that all have their own unique character. Some are vain, some are cheeky, and others live their life on a string.

Jewellery is shown life-size. This page, top: *The Little Pierrot*, 70 x 70 mm (2¾ x 2¾ in). Opposite page, top: *The Pierrot*, 133 x 108 mm (5¼ x 4¼ in). Both gold/silver-plated brass.

'My collaboration with Eva Schildt has been based on our friendship and curiosity about how we could influence each other's work.'

Maja Sten, My Little Drama

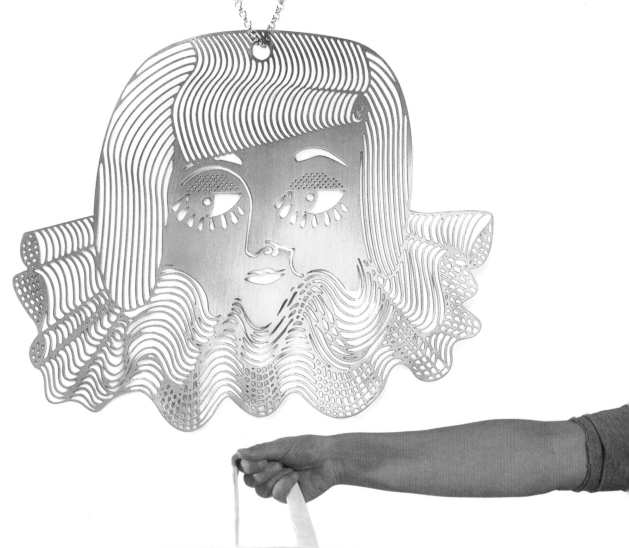

Sue Doeksen |
suedoeksen.nl

Freelance illustrator Sue Doeksen works from her studio in Utrecht, the Netherlands. Since graduating in 2006 she has worked for a wide range of clients and collaborated with animators and media designers alongside self-initiated projects such as her hand screen-printed *Love Bird* shopping bags.

Vier5 | V5FD
vier5.de
fairytale-magazine.com
vier5.de/fashiondepartment
v5-warehouse.com

Left, top: Vier5's black heart motif that is applied to wall-paintings or, as in this case, to a black brooch – shown here at life-size, 102 x 97 mm (4 x 3¾ in) – which was released as part of the 2007 men's fashion collection by V5FD – Vier5's Fashion Department.

Opposite page: Excerpt from Vier5's *Fairy Tale* magazine from winter 2006, featuring the heart brooch.

Left, bottom: The jute bags by Vier5 go back to the green and peace movements of the late 1970s and early 1980s. At the time, slogans such as '*Schwerter zu Pflugscharen*' (swords into ploughshares) or '*Jutte statt Plastik*' (jute instead of plastic) were printed on these bags in Germany. The rough material, resembling agricultural sacks, contrasted with plastic materials that were then already deemed dangerous and harmful to the environment. The jute bag didn't survive the changing times, but plastic bags did. Yet one successor of the jute bag is the fabric or paper bag that is still used today.

'Even when we were still students we used to work on our own projects already and since then some of those have occasionally reappeared in different forms. Our "mouse-face", for instance, is one of them – it's over 10 years old now – and it has resurfaced every year in another form.'

Marco Fiedler and Achim Reichert, Vier5

Peepshow | Peepshop

peepshow.org.uk
peepshop.org.uk

Top: Peepshow collective's series of laser-cut acrylic pieces from 2006, including: this page, top: *Stag Boy Decoration* by Chrissie Macdonald;
opposite page, left to right from top: *Think & Do Bird Decoration* by Jenny Bowers, *Horse Decoration* and *Woodland Decoration* by Chrissie Macdonald, *Jewel 2 Decoration* by Lucy Vigrass, *Robot Decoration* by Andrew Rae, *Ghost Keyring* by Luke Best and *Skull Decoration* by Andrew Rae, which was also produced as a keyring. All laser-cut acrylic pieces were released in editions of 30.

Bottom, left to right: Series of screen-printed shopping bags from 2008 that includes the *Meccano Bag (Yellow)* by Lucy Vigrass, *Bird In The Hand Bag* by Spencer Wilson, *X Ray Bag* by Andrew Rae and two screen-printed tote bags from 2005: *Leaf Bag* by Jenny Bowers and *Ghost Bag* by Luke Best. All bags were released in editions of 30.

'We also get plenty of orders from people who commission us commercially; we had most of the art directors and assistants from the Saturday Telegraph *round our studio once, buying up Christmas presents.'*
Miles Donovan, Peepshow

Miscellaneous |

This must be one of our favourite chapters. It contains a particularly rich mix, including skateboard decks, furniture, pillows, stickers, mugs, plates, tapes, notebooks, tea towels, music and fine art editions, sculptures and CCTV cameras, hunting trophies, cuckoo clocks and pets made from paper and cardboard. There is even a heat-sensitive toilet seat and a gigantic beanbag. And – we promise – every single piece was made with love!

Emily Forgot | Forgot Shop
emilyforgot.co.uk

Emily Forgot is the appropriately curious moniker of London-based designer and illustrator Emily Alston. Since graduating from Liverpool School of Art and Design in 2004, Emily Forgot has developed her own interdisciplinary visual language which embraces the odd, the everyday and the sometimes surreal. She is currently in the process of further developing her own range of products, which are available online at her Forgot Shop, as well as taking on commercial projects for clients large and small. Her plates were first exhibited in a show called 'Six Impossible Things Before Breakfast' and have gone on to show in the 'Fragiles' show at Miami Art Basel, Belgium, and most recently Dubai.

'I love the idea of my imagery being used in editorials as much as it occupying the space on someone's clothing or mantelpiece. Design always had its appeal for this reason. It can exist in so many disguises.'

Emily Alston, Emily Forgot/Forgot Shop

Maja Sten and Eva Schildt | My Little Drama

mylittledrama.com
majasten.se
evaschildt.se

Illustrator Maja Sten and product designer Eva Schildt created this collaborative piece for an exhibition in Tokyo called 'Forest Tales'. The two Swedes played with its proportion, making the acorn larger than life-size. This cast iron piece weighs 3.5 kg (7¾ lb) and is not suitable for squirrels, but works well for people who need a doorstop, bookend or weight. The two designers launched their sister company My Little Drama in 2008, where they showcase and sell their collaborative jewellery – as featured on pages 178–79.

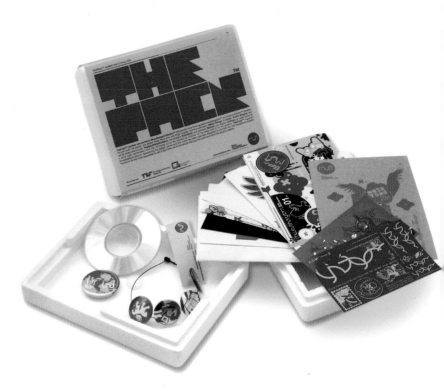

Musa |

musaworklab.com
nlfmagazine.com

Musa released several issues of their *ThePack* goodies that could include anything from limited-edition T-shirts to badges and postcards, along with works by selected collaborators. *ThePack* was released in editions of 200.

Above: *ThePack01* included work by Musa and RMAC, Dialetica, Vector Brigade, Niponik and Feliciano Type Foundry.

Below: *ThePack02 – PinkAddiction* contained work by Musa together with Niponik, DC/Electroclandestino, Jucapinga and Passvite.

Opposite page: Musa's self-initiated *HoleMug* project was first presented at Portuguese design biennale Experimenta Design in 2005. The mugs were then customized by selected artists and were displayed in an exhibition that took place in the HoldMe store in Lisbon. The travelling exhibition then moved to other cities together with the annual 'MusaTour' exhibitions.

TheHoleMug was designed by Musa in collaboration with product designers Jorge Trindade and João Seco. Artists who created one-off custom mugs included Dialetica, Jucapinga, Niponik, Vector Brigade, MissCMYK, Nelson Araújo, DC/Electroclandestino, Talita Romão, Conspira, Pedro Carmo and Luis Buchinho.

So far Musa has produced only a limited edition of 50 *HoleMugs* in plain white. The team is planning to make this beautiful piece commercially available in the future.

'It all started in summer 2003 when we had a dream with the ambitious objective to help promote and showcase the Portuguese design scene nationally and worldwide.'

Raquel Viana, Paulo Lima and Ricardo Alexandre, Musa

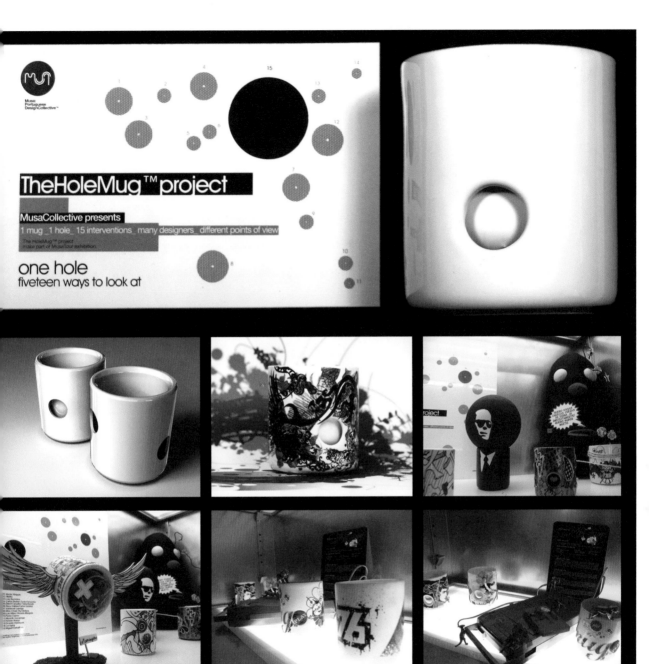

TheHoleMug™ project

MusaCollective presents

1 mug _1 hole_ 15 interventions_ many designers_ different points of view

The HoleMug™ project make part of MusaTour exhibition.

one hole
fiveteen ways to look at

Emmi Salonen |
emmi.co.uk

Finnish graphic designer Emmi Salonen
and her design studio Emmi produce
sideline projects that are available via her
online shop or from selected retailers.

Above: this beautiful Emmi mug is called
What a Day.

Opposite page: *Reused Envelope Tape*
encourages Emmi's customers and clients
to do exactly this – to recycle received
envelopes.

123Klan | Bandit-1$m
123klan.com
123klan.bigcartel.com

This mug by French graffiti artists Scien
and Klor, aka 123Klan, is from 2005. Since
2008 the pair have released their own
products via their sideline *Bandit-1$m*.

*'I think we release our own products because of our graffiti background –
we just can't stop writing our names everywhere on everything.
The cool side of goodies, though, is that you get money back from your hard work.'*
Scien and Klor, 123Klan

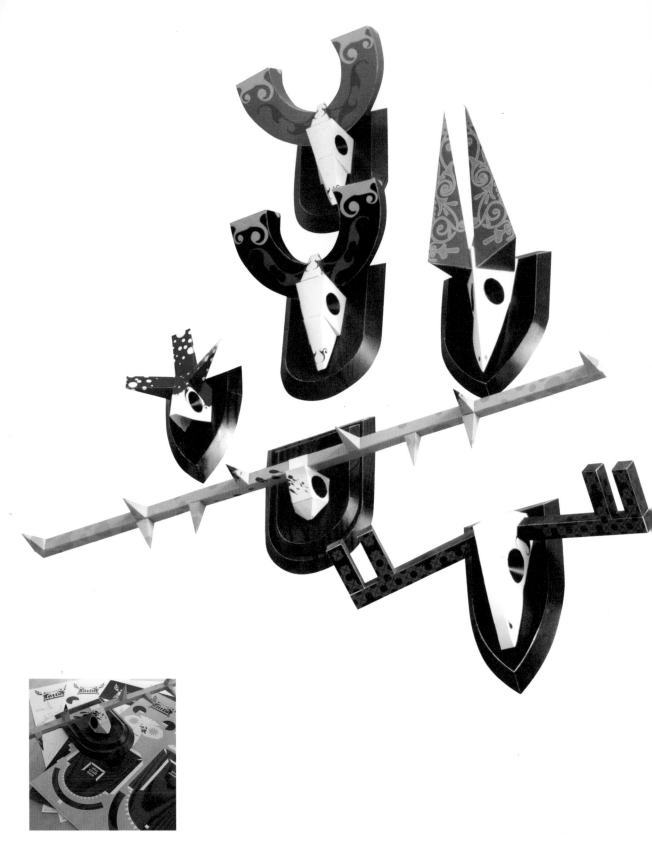

'The Antlor product was actually the start of my company. I was going to have considerable expenses producing this, so founding a company at that time made perfect sense.'
Kenn Munk

Kenn Munk |
kennmunk.com
antlor.net

Denmark-based graphic designer Kenn Munk set up his own studio in 2005 and frequently releases self-initiated projects, such as his paper kits *Antlor – The Deer Departed* and his *Sniptape*.

Opposite page: *Antlor – The Deer Departed* are paper kits that can be cut out and, having constructed them, his customers have hunting trophies to hang on the wall of their den, hunting cabin or glorious cubicle. The kits come in three different designs, limited to 2,000 numbered prints of each design, packed in ziplock bags. *Antlor* kits also include a blank, customizable DIY version. *Antlor – The Deer Departed* was released in 2005.

Above: *Sniptape* is 66m (216ft) of cut-out-ability. It's a joke in the form of adhesive tape: it's the fastest way to convert your ride into a convertible; it's the fastest way to add a new doorway to your house; the fastest way to make anything a coupon to cut out and take to the store…

Garudio Studiage |
garudiostudiage.com

Garudio Studiage is a London-based creative collective set up by graphic designer and *Flat Pets* creator Chris Ratcliffe, together with Laura Cave, Anna Walsh and Hannah Havana. *Flat Pets* kitten, puppy and rabbit are available at Garudio Studiage's online shop. They are screen-printed and die-cut A4 sheets of 1000 gsm recycled grey board and come with attached stand.

'It is really nice to know that people want to buy things that we have made just because we wanted to rather than someone else asking us to do it.'

Chris Ratcliffe, Garudio Studiage

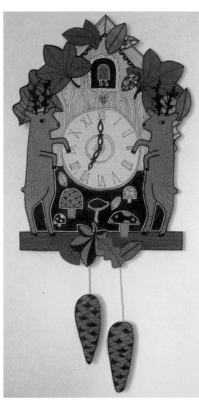

Kate Sutton |
katesutton.co.uk
katesutton.etsy.com

These beautiful cuckoo clocks by British illustrator Kate Sutton were originally for an exhibition in the US that she took part in. After posting pictures of the clocks on her blog she received a lot of enquiries asking whether she would make any more – and so she did.

Peter Crnokrak, The Luxury of Protest |
theluxuryofprotest.com

Before becoming a graphic designer Peter Crnokrak was a researcher in the sciences – specifically, quantitative genetics. While in design school he started producing self-initiated projects to sell in stores in Montréal such as his *Thermochromic Toilet Seat*, an object with memory that retains the mark of the previous user.

Crnokrak writes: 'In a way, objects can tell a story of their serial use over time. Often such historical marks are undesirably manifest as scratches, dents or general wear. Very rarely are objects expressly designed to record and communicate the manner of their use over time.'

The acrylic toilet seat was impregnated with heat-sensitive plastisol ink that changes colour from a deep reddish orange when cold, to bright yellow when warmed to the temperature of a body – 36°C (97°F). The seat gives people an idea about what to expect when they sit down, enhancing the experience of using public bathrooms.

'Self-initiated work shows the world what can be achieved when economics and restraint are thrown out the window – when the designer is simply left to go to it. When all that's left is pure motivation, the results can be startlingly poignant.'

Peter Crnokrak, The Luxury of Protest

Peepshow | Peepshop
peepshow.org.uk
peepshop.org.uk

Peepshow collective created a series of tea towels in 2008 including (left to right) *Vessels Tea Towel* and *House Tea Towel* by Jenny Bowers, *Magpie Tea Towel* by Spencer Wilson and *Buttons Tea Towel* by Lucy Vigrass.

They were all screen-printed on 100 per cent natural unbleached cotton tea towels, measuring 500 x 800 mm (19¾ x 31½ in).

Alex Robbins |
alexrobbins.co.uk

Alex Robbins is a freelance illustrator and graphic designer. His flat-pack *CCTV Kits* from 2006 were originally created for an exhibition at a warehouse in Dalston, London. Three CCTV cameras were positioned around the warehouse, with the flat-pack kit available to purchase beneath one of the cameras. The project questions whether CCTV is an effective way to tackle crime. As you build the cardboard kit, information and statistics about security cameras are positioned on the gluing and folding areas. The remaining kits – only an edition of 25 – were then placed around the city or sold via his website when it launched.

'*Since setting up my business I have worked for companies based all around the world. I still find it amazing that I have yet to meet a client face to face.*'
Alex Robbins

I LIKE IT,
WHAT
IS IT?

TOMORROW

Anthony Burrill |
anthonyburrill.com

Freelance designer Anthony Burrill originally made the *Open/Closed* design (right) a long time ago as a postcard but decided to remake it in 2008 as a facsimile of an actual shop sign. It was first sold in KK Outlet, a gallery/shop/office in Hoxton Square, London. The sign is also used on the door of their shop, confusing everybody who visits. The shop sign was screen-printed in an edition of 500.

Above: *Tomorrow Pads*, from 2006, were made as part of a series of products under the name *Tomorrow* in collaboration with Jethro Marshall. The notebooks were the most successful part of the project. The pads were letterpress-printed in an edition of 300. Initial quantities were sold in Colette, Paris. There are plans to relaunch the *Tomorrow* brand soon.

'I think it can be really helpful to show companies that an idea can work by actually making it first, proving it sells and that there's interest in it.'

Jon Burgerman

Jon Burgerman |
jonburgerman.com

Jon Burgerman has built a strong reputation through his unique and colourful artworks of swooping, intertwining lines and hyper-emotional characters. Working across a variety of media that includes drawing, painting, print, animation, large-scale murals and toy design, his art retains a handmade, hand-drawn quality.

Opposite page: *Bunny Flop* is a collaboration between Burgerman and Martin Vicker. Conceived in a backstreet alley (above a tea room with great carrot cake) *Bunny Flop* is an Oldenburgian soft-sculpture beanbag that fuses the furniture and interior design expertise of Martin Vicker with Burgerman's character doodles. The *Bunny Flop* has been set up around UK galleries and design festivals. This self-initiated project will lead to further multiples of smaller *Bunny Flops* in the future.

Left: Stickers were the first product Burgerman ever produced. The packs are sold on his site and by a few select retailers around the globe.

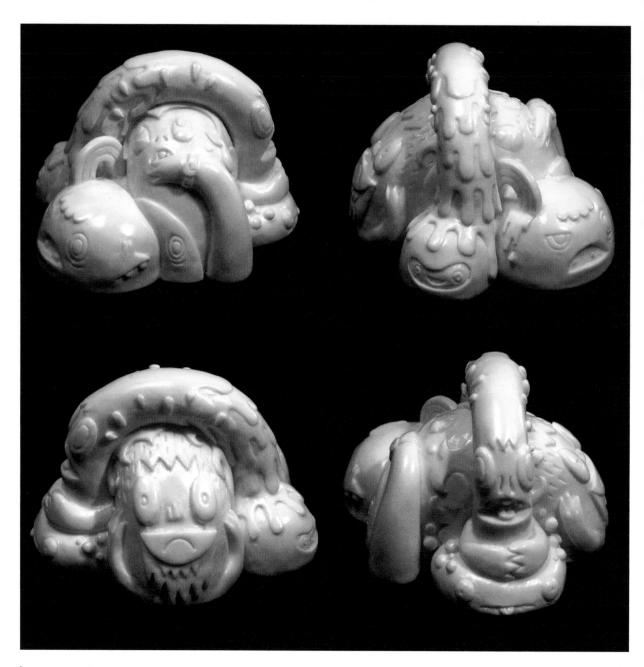

Approximately 135 x 120 x 80 mm (9¼ x 4¾ x 3¼ in)

*'Originally I wanted to generate a little extra income.
Later on I thought I'd make a few things myself just to see how they'd go,
rather than wait for someone to invite me to make them and just to have complete
control over the work. This is especially true of the sculpture Worryknott.'*

Jon Burgerman

Jon Burgerman |
jonburgerman.com

Opposite page: *Worryknott* is a limited-edition desktop sculpture designed by Jon Burgerman and sculpted by Stu Witter. The editions of 50 each were produced locally in Nottingham, UK, and come signed, numbered and with an exclusive enamel badge. The sculpture is Burgerman's first attempt at capturing one of his intertwined doodles in a three-dimensional form. Shapes and faces overlap while the contours run smoothly across different shapes as they would in his traditional two-dimensional work.

Left: *Pop Idols* are large sculptures made from expanded polystyrene and have a resin shell, so they are light and can withstand a slight knock. The blue one is titled *Walla (Keeper of Pies and Snacks variant)*, the yellow one is titled *Leona (Three Horned Vengeful variant)* and the pink one is titled *Ray (Homunculus Fully Grown variant)*. The set were exhibited in a couple of his exhibitions, including a solo show in Beijing.

700 x 1,060 mm (27⅝ x 41¾ in) |

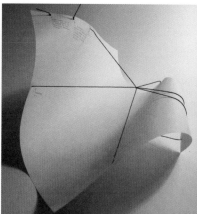

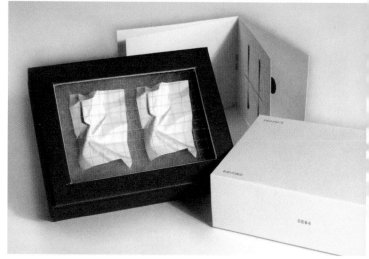

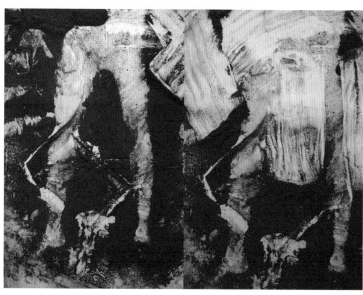

Rick Myers | Subscription Editions
footprintsinthesnow.co.uk

Based in Manchester, UK, and Massachusetts, USA, Rick Myers' works are included in special collections at The British Library, The Poetry Library in London, MoMA New York and Tate Britain. In 2007 he launched 'Subscription Editions' – an annual series of limited-edition booklets, prints, objects and unique artworks sent to subscribers by post.

This page: 'Subscription Editions' (SE) issues one, three and four from 2007 and followed at the bottom by a detail from issue six. From top left: SE #1: *Bite Marks in Paper*; SE #3: *Inert Publication*; SE #4: *ProjectxRecordxRecordxProjectxProjectx-Recordx-RecordxProjectxProject*.

Opposite page: SE #5: *Expedition Into Page (Prologue)*, 2006–2008 and SE #6: *Untitled Document + Residue*, 2006–2008.

'Releasing objects by subscription allows quite short deadlines; it's a challenge, making multiples with such cost, size and weight limitations; straining out any superfluous material.'

Rick Myers

Artiva Design | Artiva Shop

artiva.it
artiva.it/shop

Genoa-based studio Artiva Design was founded by Daniele De Batté and Davide Sossi in 2003. One of their many self-initiated works is a CD called *Ennui* published in an edition of 25 between 2007 and 2008. Each CD is a one-off piece featuring individual 15-minute ambient soundtracks by the team. All 25 releases come in individually designed 12-inch vinyl-sized sleeves based on the 25 illustrations shown here on the right. Artiva projects like this one are available from their online shop.

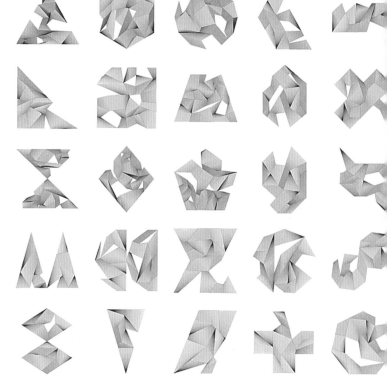

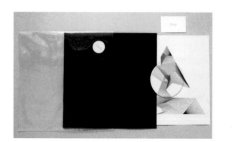

'We're very fond of arts and music and these passions very often are an inspiration for our work.'

Davide Sossi and Daniele De Batté, Artiva Design

Judith Egger | Edition Graphon
judithegger.com
editiongraphon.com

Artist and designer Judith Egger is a graduate of the Royal College of Art, London, and is now based in Munich, Germany, where she launched Edition Graphon in 2003.

Left: *Graphon 03 – Script Liechen*, 2005. It features a field recording by Loren Chasse and design by Egger herself.

Below: *Graphon 04 – Short Frites A / Short Frites AA with a double mini-CD*, 2004/2006, featuring composer Anselm Caminada, with a cardboard box and fluorescent screen-print artwork by graphic designer Anja Gerscher.

Graphon is also available as a subscription.

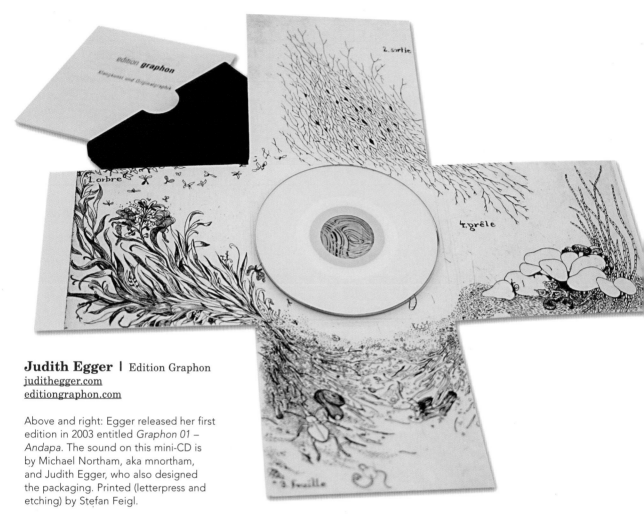

Judith Egger | Edition Graphon

judithegger.com
editiongraphon.com

Above and right: Egger released her first edition in 2003 entitled *Graphon 01 – Andapa.* The sound on this mini-CD is by Michael Northam, aka mnortham, and Judith Egger, who also designed the packaging. Printed (letterpress and etching) by Stefan Feigl.

Opposite page: *Graphon 02 – Shadowgraph* from 2004 features London-based composer Dan Carey and Egger's design. Printed (letterpress) by Stefan Feigl. Laser-cut by Kremo, Germany.

'I like to be able to distribute ideas and stories in bigger quantities than having just one original piece of artwork. I also enjoy collaborating with and featuring fellow artists who I admire for what they do. It is a wonderful way of getting to know them.'

Judith Egger, Edition Graphon

Brighten the Corners |

brightenthecorners.com

These six different *Notebooks* by Billy Kiosoglou
and Frank Philippin, who run Brighten the Corners,
were released in 2008 and are available via their
website. Folded down, they measure 121 x 195 mm
(4¾ x 7¾ in), are stapled twice and trimmed with
a gold cut to the side. The main idea behind them
was to reduce the elements of a notebook as much
as possible and see what's left.

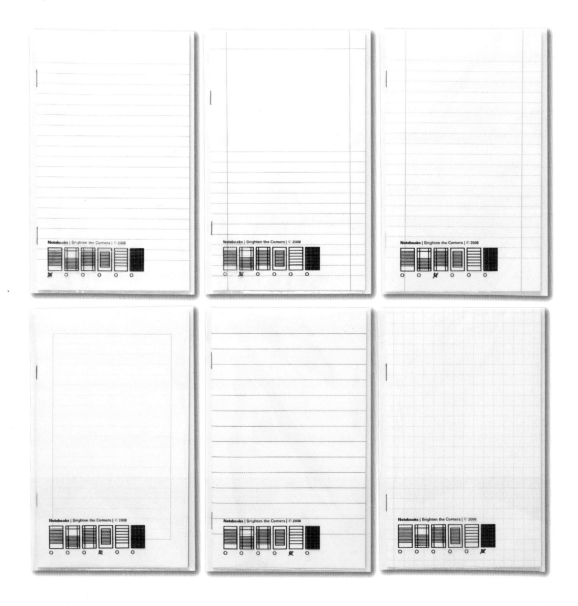

*'The notebooks came out of an existing project we were working on, which
we decided would be nice to produce for ourselves. So it was literally created "on the side"
since the printer printed the job and then continued running the press for our notebooks.'*

Billy Kiosoglou, Brighten the Corners

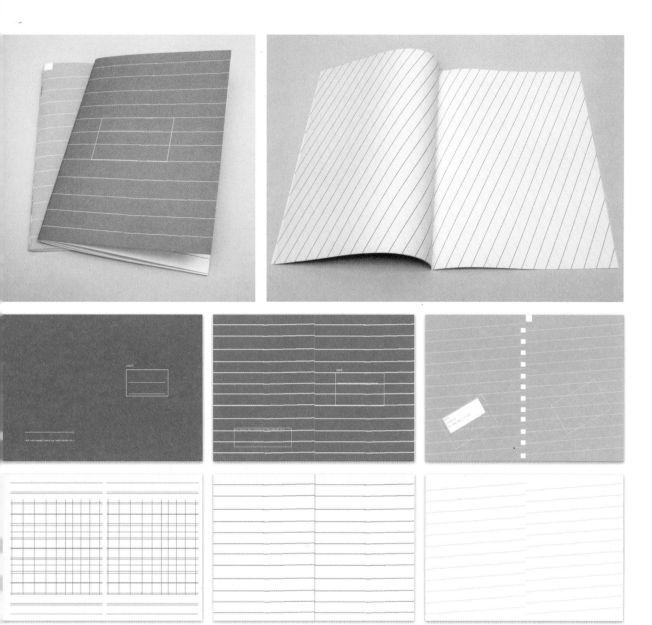

Vier5 |

vier5.de
fairytale-magazine.com
vier5.de/fashiondepartment
v5-warehouse.com

Vier5's *Exercise Books* attract attention not only with their colours but also with their insides. The lines are not designed as usual. Due to some slight interferences by Vier5, these exercise books offer new modes of use.

Astrid Stavro | The Art of the Grid
astridstavro.com
artofthegrid.com

Italian-born Astrid Stavro runs her own design studio SAS (Studio Astrid Stavro) in Barcelona. In addition to the studio, SAS also runs El Palace Editions, El Palace Exhibitions and El Palace Products, a small, self-initiated publishing company that explores ideas and their visual offspring.

Above: A self-initiated project by Stavro is *Grid-it! notepads*, which were initially developed and produced during her last two weeks at the Royal College of Art. The first *Art of the Grid* shelving units were also produced during that period.

Grid-it! notepads are a series of notepads based on the layout grids of famous publications. They are a selection of grids that have played a historic role in the development of design systems, covering a wide spectrum of classic and contemporary editorial design.

There are seven notepads in total. Left to right from top: *The Guardian* newspaper (David Hillman, 1988), *The Gutenberg Bible* (Johannes Gutenberg, 1455), *Twen* magazine (Willy Fleckhaus, 1959), *Die neue Typographie* (Jan Tschichold, 1928), *Raster Systeme* (Josef Müller-Brockmann, 1981), *A Designer's Art* (Paul Rand, 1985) and *Le Modulor* (Le Corbusier, 1948).

Opposite page: *Grid-it! notepads* have extended into *The Art of the Grid* products which include shelving units and cutting mats. The shelving units take the *Grid-it! notepads* a step further by transforming the grids into three-dimensional products and taking them into the realm of industrial and product design.

'It is difficult to juggle studio work and self-initiated projects at the same time…
However, finding the time for self-initiated projects is crucial.'
Astrid Stavro

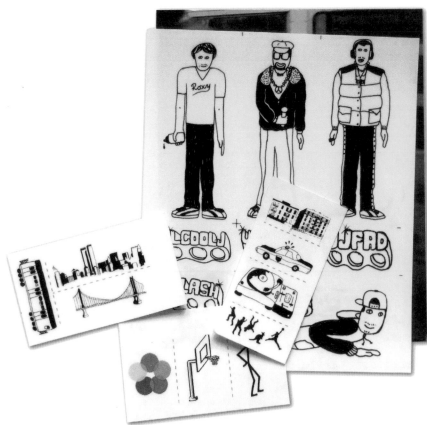

Bureau l'Imprimante |

wmaker.net/imprimante
limprimante.myshopify.com

French graphic designer Loïc Boyer runs Bureau l'Imprimante from Rouen where he publishes his books, zines and products.

Left: A bag of translucent stickers from an edition of 120, digital print on adhesive paper, 120 x 240 mm (4¾ x 9⅜ in).

Below: *Un Aimant Aimant* – a magnet for Japan lovers (and Pushpin Studio lovers, too), 87 x 50 mm (3⅜ x 2 in), print on high-quality vinyl, and next to it (below left) a magnet starring the *Ultramagnetic MCs*, 107 x 140 mm (4¼ x 5½ in), print on high-quality vinyl.

'The first place I look for on a designer's website is the shop section. That's where you can see the real thing.'

Loïc Boyer, Bureau l'Imprimante

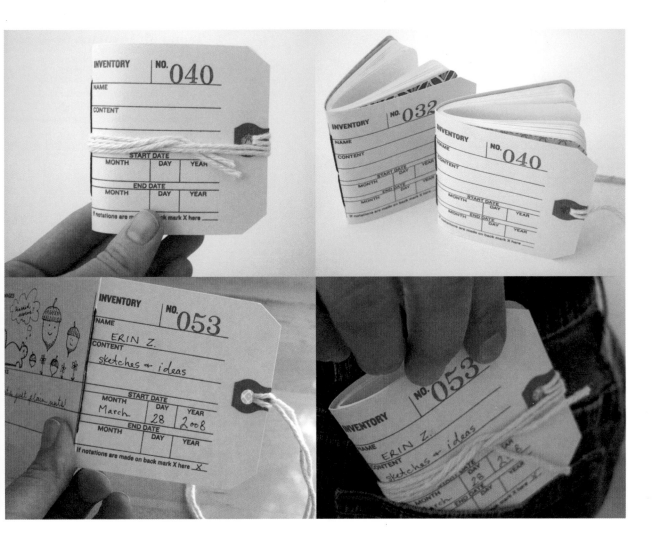

Erin Zamrzla |
erinzam.com
erinzam.etsy.com

Designer, bookbinder and artist Erin Zamrzla is based
in Santa Monica, California where she runs her own
design studio, freelances and takes on commissioned
work. The majority of her projects are sold online.
Shown here is her hand screen-printed *Mini Tag
Book – Inventory Edition*. Each book is stamped with
its own inventory number and is filled with 100 pages.
Half of these are blank (unlined), acid-free sketch
paper, and these alternate with wide-ruled pages.
Finished size is 80 x 80 mm (3¼ x 3¼ in). The pages
are hand-bound with pamphlet stitch binding in red
linen thread.

Tamar Moshkovitz, Go-Tam |
go-tam.com

Tel Aviv-based Tamar Moshkovitz is a freelance designer, illustrator and animator, and created *Plushood* plush dolls and animation with partner Shlomi Schillinger. Sometimes she even finds time for her own projects, like this brilliant *Ahoy!* postcard.

Home de Caramel |
homedecaramel.com

Multi-disciplinary studio Home de Caramel was set up near Barcelona in 2008. These small plastic lights in different colours are intended for kids and fun-loving adults. They were produced in a limited edition of 50.

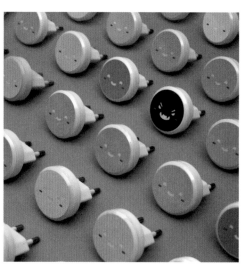

'We are an animation and graphic design studio, but we like to design funny objects whenever possible.'
Jordi, Home de Caramel

GELUKSPAS
INVINCIBLE IN 2008

VALID UNTIL 31·12·08

OWNER: TOMI

VALID UNTIL 31-12-08

AGATHE

BITE

SUE

GELUKSPAS

VALID TILL
31·12·'07

OWNER:

MARTIJN

Sue Doeksen |
suedoeksen.nl

Dutch freelance illustrator Sue Doeksen
has been making *Good Luck Passes*
for friends and family since 2003. Now
many other people carry them in their
wallets and long for the next edition.
Every year the orders for her *Good Luck
Passes* increase.

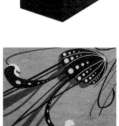

Lucas Richards and Adam Leick | Mouse Saw
mousesaw.com

Mouse Saw is a US-based collaboration between graphic designer Lucas Richards and furniture designer Adam Leick. Together they recently started to create screen-printed furniture – functional pieces of art.

'All our pieces are a labour of love.'
Lucas Richards, Mouse Saw

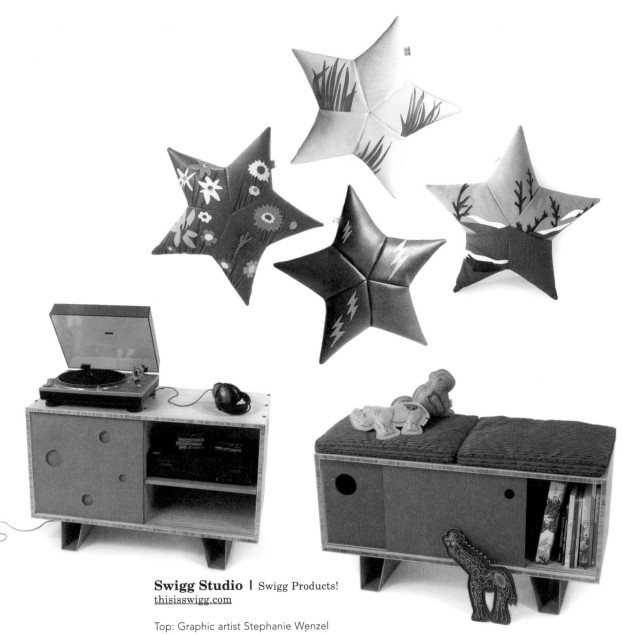

Swigg Studio | Swigg Products!
thisisswigg.com

Top: Graphic artist Stephanie Wenzel received a 1950s Singer sewing machine from her grandmother and started playing around with it. The first line of products she created were five-pointed pillows called *SwiggStars!* that were an extension of the pieces created for a group art show called the 'WCOS Pillow Show and Sale' at the Riviera Gallery in Brooklyn, New York.

Above: *Pandabox Collection, Big Twin Cub* and *Little Twin Cub* were created in collaboration with Curt Meissner at Small Factory Design.

1201am |
1201am.com

Laurie Forehand is a graphic designer currently working in Atlanta, Georgia, where she runs her own brand and design studio 1201am. Shown here are her *Home Decorativ* pillows that she sells alongside other products on her website.

HunterGatherer |
huntergatherer.net
greenlady.com

Right and opposite page: The woodgrain-pattern pillow, wallet, magazine rack and skateboard deck were designed and produced by designer Gary Benzel and artist, designer and film-maker Todd St. John. Together the two initiated Green Lady, an influential clothing and product line in 1994. In 2000 St. John set up studio/workshop HunterGatherer in New York.

'I think creatives have always done sideline work for themselves.
It's in our nature to design and create, and technology has advanced to make this work faster,
and more enjoyable, while also giving us more tools to make it easier to apply our designs
to new materials and create more tangible products.'
Laurie Forehand, 1201am

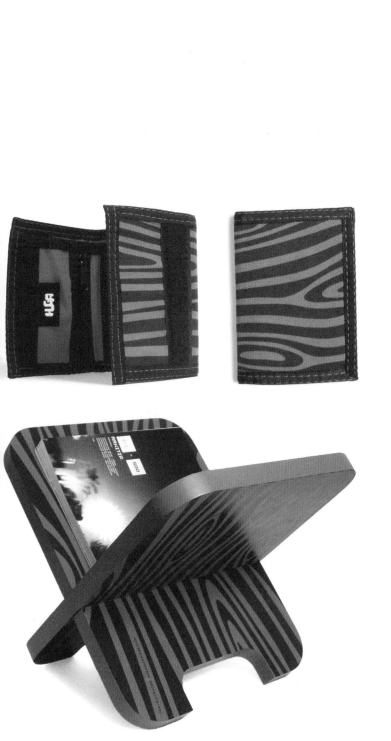

Platform Skateboarding |

platformboards.co.uk
splendid-industrial.co.uk

UK-based Platform is the creative outlet of designers Jeremy Owen and Chris Carus, who both also have separate day jobs. One of them works in exhibition design, the other in publishing.

Their *Tricorn* skateboard deck is a *hommage* to the controversial Tricorn Centre that was built in Portsmouth, UK, in 1966. This multi-purpose shopping centre was a classic example of Brutalist architecture. Although appreciated by some – its vast expanses of ultra-smooth tarmac, painted kerbs and loading bays made it a skateboard heaven – it was voted Britain's fourth-ugliest building in 1968, neglected over decades and torn down in 2004.

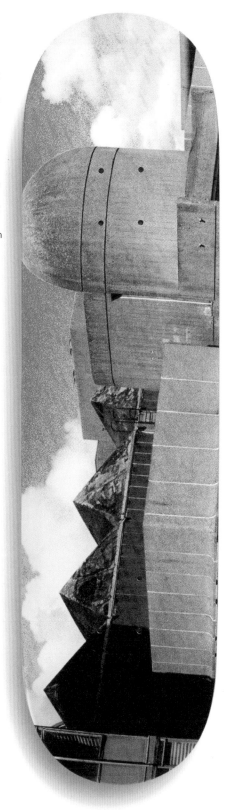

'Undeniably, the technical and creative opportunities that arise from our experiences in the professional environment (ie our day jobs) inform and instruct the work we do as Platform. The reverse is also true, though to a lesser extent.'

Jeremy Owen and Chris Carus, Platform

TADO |
tado.co.uk

Laser-etched skateboard deck by
Sheffield-based Mike and Katie at TADO.
The deck was created for a 2007 group
show at The WindUp Gallery.

'An equation for the people who strive for what they believe in.
Motivation + Creation = Satisfaction.'

Matt Jones and Afshin Shahi

Lunartik JOnes |
lunartik.com
lunartikshop.bigcartel.com
un-plugged.co.uk
flickr.com/groups/un-plugged

Un-plugged by British artist Matt Jones, aka Lunartik JOnes, is an ongoing project started in 2002 which highlights the possible loss of power that humanity will one day face. Over seven years, 20 countries, and 40,000 stickers, the *un-plugged* project is well underway. See the *un-plugged* stickers in action on the next page.

Opposite page: Besides the *un-plugged* stickers, Lunartik also created large, limited-edition canvases, 420 x 420 mm (16½ x 16½ in) as shown here, as well as large poster versions and fabric patches.

'The number of large businesses that are being inspired by personal projects –
be it street art or design – proves that we hold the power to shape the future.
It's a very exciting time.'

Matt Jones, Lunartik JOnes

Loop the Loop

Mind the Gap!

Ambush

Abduction

Terminal 5

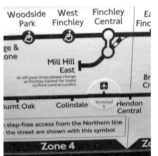

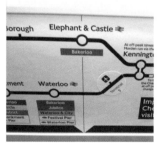

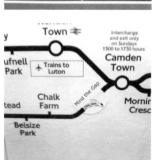

Lunartik JOnes |
lunartik.com
lunartikshop.bigcartel.com
un-plugged.co.uk
flickr.com/groups/un-plugged

Opposite page: *Un-plugged* stickers by Lunartik JOnes, as presented on the previous two pages. Pictures are sent back to Lunartik by his global customer base.

This page: The *Northern Line Sticker Campaign* is one of Lunartik's ongoing projects since 2002. These cheeky stickers can be found hiding on tube maps, in the Northern Line train carriages on the London Underground. Though the stickers are small, they are highly effective at bringing a smile to the faces of Londoners.

Contributor Profiles |

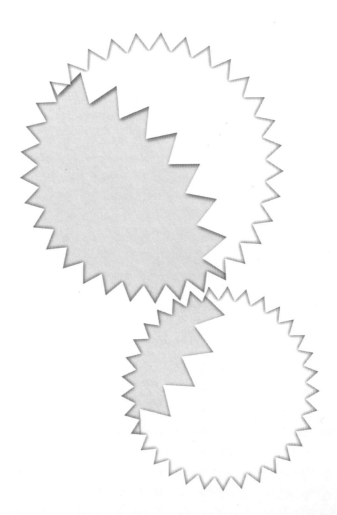

1201am |
1201am.com

Laurie Forehand is a graphic designer currently working in Atlanta, Georgia. As a New Year's goal in January 2000, Laurie began the online design studio and brand 1201am. Focusing on innovation in design, the site showcases online projects and digital artwork created by talented designers from around the globe. The site is an open area for artists to display their work and share industry trends and information. In recent years, 1201am has featured a new line of paper goods and housewares in Laurie's signature design style.

123Klan |
123klan.com
123klan.bigcartel.com

Mr and Mrs Jacob, aka Scien and Klor, have been graffiti artists since 1989. 123Klan were the first to blend graffiti writing and graphic art. Formerly based in France, they now live and work in Montréal, Canada, where they continue their creative mix of commissioned and self-initiated projects. Their monograph was published in 2004 and an updated version was released in 2007 by French publisher Pyramyd Editions.

A

Add Fuel To The Fire |
addfueltothefire.com
addfueltothefire.com/shop
ignitedclothing.com

Ignited clothing is Diogo Machado's playground brand with exclusive artwork from his studio Add Fuel To The Fire, based in Portugal. Ignited was launched in 2007.

Airside |
airside.co.uk
airsideshop.com
brassier.blogspot.com

Founded in 1999, Airside is a London-based design company. The people of Airside come from different disciplines, ranging from computer programming and English literature to textiles and graphic design, as well as clubs and music. Enjoyment and passion are the prerequisites for all Airside's work – be it websites, animation, T-shirts or CD sleeves. Anne Brassier has been with Airside since 2001 and handles all press, marketing and new business matters. Anne is mother to the Stitches – woolly creatures adopted into new homes via Airside's online shop.

Paulo Arraiano |
pauloarraiano.com
palmshirts.com

Paulo Arraiano, aka Yup, co-founded Palm in Portugal, together with Leonor Morais. Palm is a brand intended to serve as a forum for experimentation in Portuguese design, illustration, street art and for international collaborations.

Artiva Design |
artiva.it
artiva.it/shop
takeshape.it
danieledebatte.it

Genoa-based studio Artiva Design was founded in 2003 by Daniele De Batté and Davide Sossi. The studio works across many media, including web design, illustration, typography, photography and graphic design. De Batté and Sossi also work on independent projects including their patterns collection, takeshape.it.

Atelier télescopique |
ateliertelescopique.com
ainsifont.com
wassingue.com

Stéphane Meurice, Sébastien Delobel, Xavier Meurice, Guillaume Berry and Baptiste Servais make up Lille-based design studio Atelier télescopique. Two of their self-initiated projects are Wassingue – Floor Clothes Design – and their digital typeface foundry Ainsi Font where their font creations are available online. Wassingue is a clothing brand created in 2003 with a first T-shirt collection released for the general public in early 2008.

Craig Atkinson |
craigatkinson.co.uk
caferoyal.org

British artist Craig Atkinson has a masters in Fine Art, in which he also teaches and lectures. Until fairly recently he made big, abstract, very formal paintings, but has now returned to drawing, his work focusing on the everyday and the absurd. Since returning to drawing he has accidentally been working as an illustrator but still considers himself a fine artist. In 2008 he released Reward – a collection of selected drawings from his sketchbook pages that was published by Café Royal – his family-run online shop and offline publishing house specializing in artists' books and zines.

B

Brighten the Corners |
brightenthecorners.com

Billy Kiosoglou and Frank Philippin run Brighten the Corners, an independent, multi-disciplinary design and strategy consultancy with offices in London and Stuttgart. Established in 1999, the small organization handles both large- and small-scale projects. Whether designing a book or a stamp or branding an organization, their designs focus on clear and direct communication.

Stefan G. Bucher, 344 |
344design.com
dailymonster.com

Stefan G. Bucher, originally from Germany, is based in California where he runs his design studio, 344. He is an award-winning designer and author, a monster illustrator, and the Art Directors Club of New York even declared him a Young Gun in 2004. Bucher is the creator of the incredibly popular dailymonster.com and the author of the companion book and DVD *100 Days of Monsters*.

Bureau l'Imprimante |
wmaker.net/imprimante
limprimante.myshopify.com

Graphic designer Loïc Boyer, a graduate from La Sorbonne's Art Department, has run Bureau l'Imprimante in Rouen since 2001, where he publishes his books, zines and products. In 2006 a series of artists' books, made in collaboration with photographer Yveline Loiseur, became part of the public collection of the FRAC Haute-Normandie. He also regularly publishes a free fanzine called *Crocodile*.

Jon Burgerman |
jonburgerman.com
biro-web.com

British artist Jon Burgerman has built a strong reputation through his unique and colourful artworks of swooping, intertwining lines and hyper-emotional characters. Working across a variety of media that includes drawing, painting, print, animation, large-scale murals and toy design, his art retains a handmade, hand-drawn quality. Burgerman currently lives in Nottingham, in the East Midlands of the UK. In 2008 IdN released the book *Jon Burgerman: Pens are My Friends* – the first ever publication to feature his commercial, personal and collaborative works alongside each other.

Anthony Burrill |
anthonyburrill.com

Anthony Burrill studied graphic design at Leeds Polytechnic before completing his Masters degree at the Royal College of Art in London. He works as a freelance designer producing print, moving-image and interactive design. His projects include poster campaigns for London Underground, Diesel, Hans Brinker Budget Hotel, Playstation, Nike and interactive web-based projects for Kraftwerk and Air. Anthony lives and works on the Isle of Oxney, Kent.

Jez Burrows |
eveningtweed.com
singstatistics.co.uk

Edinburgh-based graphic designer Jez Burrows freelances and is also a member of Sing Statistics and the collective Evening Tweed. He launched *The Modern Listener's Guide* in 2008. His popular series of large-format screen-prints marry indie rock and information graphics.

Matt Burvill, HouseOfBurvo |
houseofburvo.co.uk

HouseOfBurvo is home to all of graphic designer Matt Burvill's sidelines. It functions as portfolio, font foundry and freelance portal. HouseOfBurvo will be focusing its energies on the font foundry more and more as time goes on, as this has always been the founder's true love.

Andrew Byrom |
andrewbyrom.com

Andrew Byrom was born in Liverpool, UK. After graduating in 1997 he opened his own studio in London. Byrom moved to America in 2000 and lives in Los Angeles. He now divides his time between teaching, designing for various clients and working on his own self-initiated three-dimensional typefaces. *Grab-Me* was honoured with a Type Directors Award (TDC, New York) in 2007.

C

Ian Caulkett |
fantasticsuburbia.com
iancaulkett.net
tiptoecollective.co.uk

Caulkett is a member of Tiptoe, a London-based illustration collective that he formed with Mark Whittle and James Nicholls in 2008. His *Fantastic Suburbia* is an independently published collection of words (poems and prose) and pictures (illustrations and designs) originally created by him together with writer Sarah Remy.

CHK Design |
chkdesign.com
acmefonts.net

German-born Christian Küsters runs a London-based multi-disciplinary design studio, CHK Design, and a type foundry and platform, Acme Fonts, which he established in 1999. Acme Fonts allows Küsters to showcase products that reflect his passion for experimental typography.

Chris Clarke |
chris-clarke.co.uk

Chris Clarke is a recent graphic design graduate from the University of the West of England. Adopting the assertion 'in order to change things, we must first attain a decent understanding of them', he is interested in mediating the gap between design and the public, and exploring design's ability to facilitate and benefit social change. Clarke collaborated with Holly Lloyd in 2008 to create the *Lowercase t-shirt*.

Peter Crnokrak,
The Luxury of Protest |
theluxuryofprotest.com

Croatian-born London-based Peter Crnokrak studied biology and genetics before switching to graphic design. Crnokrak works with Nick Bell Design but also does freelance work as The Luxury of Protest (formerly ±). His self-initiated projects are best characterized as design-informed art. In most cases they are information visualization projects – computational aesthetics – but they also include object projects.

D

DGPH |
dgph.com.ar
molestown.com

Graphic designers Martin Lowenstein and Diego Vaisberg set up Argentinian design studio DGPH in 2005, where they create their own plush, vinyl and inflatable toys, prints, socks and collaborative books such as *Molestown*, 2006. Their colourful characters have appeared in illustrations published in numerous books and magazines around the world.

Sue Doeksen |
suedoeksen.nl

Freelance illustrator Sue Doeksen works from her studio in Utrecht, the Netherlands. Since graduating in 2006 she has worked for a wide range of clients and collaborated with animators and media designers – alongside self-initiated projects like her hand screen-printed *Love Bird* shopping bags or annual *Good Luck Passes*.

DTM INC |
frogbite.nl

Danny Geerlof, aka DTM INC ('Dan The Man Incorporated'), is an employed graphic designer who launched Dutch online T-shirt shop frogbite.nl in 2005, together with two of his friends.

E

Effektive |
effektivedesign.co.uk
effektiveblog.com

Graphic designer Greig Anderson graduated in 2004 with a degree in Applied Graphics and then worked at multi-disciplinary agency Curious, in Glasgow. Anderson also produces various freelance work for clients and self-initiated projects including button badges, posters and T-shirt designs under the name of Effektive, which he set up in 2007. He moved to Sydney in summer 2008 where he works at design studio There.

Alexander Egger |
satellitesmistakenforstars.com

Alexander Egger is an Italian-born Vienna-based graphic designer who also dabbles in art, writing and music. Working in different media on cultural and commercial projects, his clients include Adidas, Siemens, Designforum, Technisches Museum Wien, BMW, Burda Medien, Sony – Connect Europe, T-Mobile, Futurehouse Vienna, Design Austria, Vienna City Hall, Bundes-ministerium für Arbeit und Wirtschaft and Austrian Railways (ÖBB). His first monograph *Satellites Mistaken for Stars* is published by Gingko Press, California, and a second book *Tomorrow the future will be different than today* was released in 2008 by Rojo, Barcelona.

Judith Egger |
judithegger.com
editiongraphon.com

Royal College of Art graduate Judith Egger is an artist and designer based in Munich, Germany. She launched Edition Graphon in 2003 where she releases sound experiments in collaboration with hand-picked artists whose work she admires.

Emily Forgot |
emilyforgot.co.uk

Emily Forgot is the appropriately curious moniker of London-based designer and illustrator Emily Alston. Since graduating from Liverpool School of Art and Design in 2004, Emily Forgot has developed her own interdisciplinary visual language which embraces the odd, the everyday and the sometimes surreal. She is currently in the process of further developing her own range of products, which are available online at her Forgot Shop as well as taking on commercial projects for clients large and small.

F

FL@33 |
flat33.com
See page 240.

G

Garudio Studiage |
garudiostudiage.com

Garudio Studiage is a London-based creative collective set up by graphic designer Chris Ratcliffe, Laura Cave, Anna Walsh and Hannah Havana. When they are not too busy with commissioned work they create their own self-initiated products that are available via their online shop.

Tom Gauld |
cabanonpress.com

Royal College of Art graduate Tom Gauld is an illustrator and comic-book artist based in London. He has written and illustrated comics *Guardians of the Kingdom*, *Three very small Comics* and *Hunter & Painter* as well as producing comic stories and illustrations for various publications including *The Guardian*, *The Independent* and *The New Yorker*. Gauld runs Cabanon Press with Simone Lia, and together they have created comics *First* and *Second* which were republished as *Both* by Bloomsbury.

Gringografico |
gringografico.com
das-rheingold.de
benjamin-bartels.com

Benjamin Bartels and Max Kohler studied together in Wiesbaden, Germany, where they graduated in 2006. Their award-winning travel journal *Gringografico – on the road for food and fame!* documents over 10,000 miles of highway travel with snapshots of the everyday life of two designers. For six months and one day, they travelled along the Pan-American Highway from Canada to Peru, stopping at various ad agencies and design studios looking for work. In exchange they asked only for a bite to eat and a place to sleep.

H

Kimberly Hall |
nottene.net

Educated in fine arts at the School of the Museum of Fine Arts in Boston, and later receiving her MA in textiles at London's Central Saint Martins, Kimberly Hall works as a clothing and accessory designer, but also does freelance graphic design work and arts projects as well as self-initiated work such as her limited-edition books *2001* and *Dreambook*.

Happypets |
happypets.ch

Patrick 'Patch' Monnier, Violène Pont and Cédric Henny set up Happypets in 2000 – an experimental lab in the creative, graphic-design, image and illustration domain, based in Lausanne, Switzerland. They regularly release self-initiated products for their Happypets Products label including T-shirts, prints and *Rust*, their vinyl designer toy from 2005.

Harmonie intérieure |
harmonie-interieure.com

Fabien Barral is a freelance photographer and graphic designer based in St Bonnet Près Orcival, Auvergne, France. In 2008 he and his wife Frédérique set up Harmonie intérieure – a new sideline, which could easily become more than that. It's a workshop where the pair offer their latest range of bespoke home decoration pieces from a wide selection of posters and mounted pictures to typographic and illustrative wall stickers.

Al Heighton |
alanheighton.co.uk

Artist, designer and illustrator Al Heighton graduated with a degree in graphic design from the University of Salford, UK, in 2001. Heighton's tools include paint, pen, pencil and computer. Al has produced work for *The Guardian*, the *Big Issue*, *Dazed & Confused*, the TUC and the *Financial Times* among others.

Hello Duudle |
helloduudle.com
jonburgerman.com
duudle.dk

Hello Duudle (2004) was the first book made by UK artist Jon Burgerman in collaboration with Danish artist Sune Ehlers. The concertina book folds out to become a colourful frieze featuring their characters with biographies. In 2006 the team made a follow-up book called *Hello Duudle: The Duudleville Tales*.

Gareth Holt and William Smith |
assemblylondon.com
smithandwightman.com

Gareth Holt graduated from the Royal College of Art in 2004, and has since set up his own multi-disciplinary design studio, The-Projects, and together with fellow RCA graduate Ben Branagan he runs London-based Assembly. Holt shares a studio space with product designer William Smith from Smith&Wightman and the two collaborated to develop the FlatHat – a hybrid of a cap, beanie hat and bespoke dress hat.

Home de Caramel |
homedecaramel.com

Marc Esteban, Jordi Matosas and Oriol Rello are the founders of multi-disciplinary studio Home de Caramel, launched in 2008 and based near Barcelona. They divide their time between commissioned graphic design, illustration and animation projects and also self-initiated projects including functional plush toy creations with a twist.

HudsonBec |
hudsonbec.com
ifyoucould.co.uk
itsnicethat.com

HudsonBec is an independent design studio based in London, set up in the autumn of 2008 by Will Hudson and Alex Bec. They share a passion for design and have worked together on self-initiated project *If You Could* since 2006 and, more recently, the design site *It's Nice That*. Having worked with some of the industry's leading practitioners, HudsonBec are also keen to continue working on both art direction and curation projects. Clients include Design Event, Flowers Gallery, Nike, Pure Groove, Scarlet Projects and YCN.

HunterGatherer |
huntergatherer.net
greenlady.com

Todd St. John is an artist, designer and film-maker living in New York City. St. John produces both commercial and experimental work through HunterGatherer, the studio/workshop that he founded in 2000. St. John also co-founded the influential graphic T-shirt label Green Lady with designer Gary Benzel. *Nylon Magazine* described Green Lady as 'to the designer T-shirt world what Run-DMC is to hip hop'.

I

Riitta Ikonen |
rittaikonen.com
reisesack.de

Riitta Ikonen describes herself as an enthusiastic Finn with an interest in most things. She studied Illustration at the University of Brighton in the UK and, after working in advertising, decided to pursue a Masters degree in Communication Art and Design at the Royal College of Art in London where she graduated in 2008. Her work is concerned with the performance of images, through photography and costume design. She regularly collaborates with fellow RCA graduate Anja Schaffner – a German photographer – and between 2007 and 2008 the pair created the project *Bird and Leaf – A Sentimental Yearning.*

Intercity |
intercitydesign.com

Intercity is a London-based graphic design studio, formed in 2004 by Nick Foot, Nathan Gale and Tu Hoang. They are authors and designers of *Art & Sole*, published by Laurence King Publishing in 2008. Other self-initiated projects include T-shirt designs and badge sets for the label Badge/Button/Pin they run together with Gavin Lucas.

J

Jeremyville |
jeremyville.com

Jeremyville is an artist, product designer and animator. He wrote and produced the world's first book on designer toys, *Vinyl Will Kill*, which was published by IdN. In 2007 he participated in a group show at Colette in Paris alongside KAWS, Fafi, Futura, Mike Mills and Takashi Murakami and has initiated the *Sketchel* art satchel project. His art has been published in numerous international design books and magazines. Clients include Converse, Rossignol, Colette, Coca-Cola, MTV, Kidrobot, Refill, Graniph, Wooster Collective, Adidas, Artoyz, Domestic Vinyl, Corbis, Red Bull, Pop Cling, 55 DSL and Beck.

James Joyce, One Fine Day |
one-fine-day.co.uk

James Joyce is an artist and designer living and working in London. In 2006 he founded his own studio, One Fine Day, where he produces limited-edition prints of his work. He also undertakes commissions, and has worked for a wide range of clients, including Penguin books, Nike, *Creative Review*, Levi's, Kiehl's and Carhartt. His first solo gallery exhibition 'Drawings And Other Objects' in London's Kemistry Gallery took place in 2008 and featured a selection of personal and commissioned images.

K

Kapitza |
kapitza.com

Kapitza is a design partnership formed in London in 2004 by sisters Petra and Nicole Kapitza. Originally from southern Germany, the sisters have been living and working in London for over a decade. They focus on book design, illustration and visual identity work. In addition to their commissioned projects, they set up an online store in 2006 and have become renowned for their high-quality picture fonts and illustrations. Their 336-page *Geometric Book*, featuring graphic art and pattern fonts, was published in 2008 by German Verlag Hermann Schmidt.

Masashi Kawamura |
masa-ka.com

Masashi is an art director/writer at BBH New York. He was lured into the world of design when he became a member of Masahiko Sato Laboratory inTokyo. From there he started to work for advertising agencies such as Hakuhodo, BBH Japan, and 180 Amsterdam, where he created campaigns for global brands like Nissan, PlayStation, Levi's, AXE, and Adidas. Outside of advertising, he continues to experiment with design in media including from music videos, product designs and publications such as his *Rainbow In Your Hand* flipbook. These works have won numerous awards, such as NY ADC, ADC Tokyo, Cannes Cyber Lion, Japan Prize and Prix Danube.

Jeff Knowles |
mosjef.com

Jeff Knowles graduated with a BA (Hons) in graphic design from the University of Salford and, from there, joined Research Studios, London, in 1998. During Knowles' time at RS he handled a variety of projects, from large branding projects to publication design, packaging design, motion graphics and web design. Knowles also has a keen interest in photography and has worked for studio projects including Segment Systems, The Royal Court Theatre and Somerset House. He also has a photography collection with Font Shop's fStop Images.

Calin Kruse |
dienacht-magazine.com

Romanian-born freelance graphic designer and photographer Calin Kruse is based in Trier, Germany. In 2006 he launched small photocopied artzine *Rough* and since 2007 he has also been designer and editor of *dienacht* – a bi-annual, full-colour magazine on photography, design and subculture.

L

Lunartik JOnes |
lunartik.com
lunartikshop.bigcartel.com
un-plugged.co.uk
flickr.com/groups/un-plugged

Pinpointing exactly what Matt Jones does has never been an easy task. To be honest, he has trouble explaining it himself at times. Under the moniker of Lunartik, Matt has spent the last eight years using every weapon in his artistic arsenal, from fine art and product design to interweb trickery, stickers, vinyl toys and street art, to express his concept of self-fulfilment. The result of his efforts is a body of work that is as varied as it is fascinating. If you ever meet Mr JOnes, pop the kettle on and he'll no doubt happily run you through it all.

M

Making Do |
makingdo.org.uk

Making Do is an independent publication and a collective with a focus on the methods of producing creative work. It is conceived, edited and designed by Andrea Francke, Mary Ikoniadou, Asli Kalinoglu and Alexandre Coco – three graphic designers and one fine artist – and is published in London. Some of the collective's members are employed full-time; others work independently and occasionally collaborate on commissioned design projects. They all work on the publication in their spare time.

Medium |
mediumism.com

Medium is a creative studio based in Stockholm, which produces projects related to public space, architecture and visual culture. Projects by Medium often focus on the context of our everyday lives; the commonplace things that often go unnoticed. Medium is run by Jake Ford, Martin Frostner and Lisa Olausson.

Roderick Mills |
roderickmills.com

Since graduating from the Royal College of Art in 2001 Roderick has developed an international profile, working for various clients in many areas of illustration including publishing, corporate literature, editorial, advertising, animation and exhibition design. Besides other prizes he has also won the 'Mention Spéciale du Jury' at the Festival Nouveau Cinéma Montreál 2006 for his first film *Immortal Stories*.

Eivind Søreng Molvær |
eivindmolvaer.com

London-based Eivind Søreng Molvær was born in Norway where he studied before moving to London in 2005 to attend the BA graphic design course at Central Saint Martins. He graduated from there in 2008. His screen-printed *The Italic Poster* will hopefully only be the start of a series of equally brilliant products this talented designer offers via his website.

Julian Morey |
abc-xyz.co.uk
eklektic.co.uk

London-based graphic designer and typographer Julian Morey worked for Peter Saville Associates, where he designed graphics for New Order, Factory Records and The Haçienda. Having worked independently for over ten years, his clients include Diesel Jeans, Environ Records, Arena, Asprey, The Body Shop, KesselsKramer, London Records, Pentagram, Royal Mail and Vogue. In 1999 he founded Club-21 as an outlet for his diverse collection of digital typefaces. Frequently profiled by the design press, these contemporary fonts have been incorporated into advertising for clients such as Nike and for stamps for the Dutch PTT. Morey also established the publishing company Editions Eklektic to showcase his more personal work in silkscreen prints and greetings cards.

Jonathan Morris |
jonathanmorris.org.uk
sweetcreative.co.uk

Graphic designer Jonathan Morris created Microsea – a surreal world of digital microscopic forms – which won a prestigious competition run by Japanese design magazine *Shift*. In 2005 the project went on to form the basis of his first one-man show of digital art, 'Blend', at the CBAT Gallery in Cardiff. Creatively driven by his personal work, Jonathan's self-initiated projects provide the freedom to explore new techniques, which in turn fuel his commercial design studio Sweet, based in Wales.

Tamar Moshkovitz, Go-Tam |
go-tam.com
plushood.com

Tel Aviv-based Tamar Moshkovitz is a freelance designer, illustrator and animator, and created *Plushood* plush dolls and animation, with partner Shlomi Schillinger. Sometimes she even finds time for her own solo projects.

Mouse Saw |
mousesaw.com

Mouse Saw is a US-based collaboration between graphic designer Lucas Richards and furniture designer and Adam Leick. Together they recently started to create screen-printed furniture – functional pieces of art.

Kenn Munk |
kennmunk.com
antlor.net

Denmark-based graphic designer Kenn Munk set up his own studio in 2005 and frequently releases self-initiated projects such as his paper kits *Antlor – The Deer Departed* and his *Sniptape*.

Musa |
musaworklab.com
nlfmagazine.com

Musa was formed in October 2003 by Raquel Viana, Paulo Lima and Ricardo Alexandre. In 2004 the Lisbon-based collective of graphic designers organized the 'MusaTour' exhibition supporting the MusaBook project – the first Portuguese graphic design book ever compiled (published by IdN, Hong Kong). Projects such as *NLF Magazine*, the first Portuguese *Qee Happy* toy and their exclusive, limited merchandising goods (*ThePack*, *HoleMug*) followed. Commercial work developed by Musa-WorkLab helped to put the Portuguese design scene firmly on the map.

Rick Myers |
footprintsinthesnow.co.uk

Based in Manchester, UK, and
Massachusetts, USA, Rick Myers' works
are included in special collections at
The British Library, The Poetry Library in
London, MoMA New York and Tate Britain.
His acclaimed seven-year project, *Funnel
Vision Portable Museum* was shown both
at the 2004 Liverpool Biennial and during
British Architecture Week in Birmingham
in 2005. In 2007 he launched Subscription
Editions – an annual series of limited-
edition booklets, prints, objects and
unique artworks sent to subscribers
by post.

My Little Drama |
mylittledrama.com
majasten.se
evaschildt.se

Product designer Eva Schildt and
illustrator Maja Sten launched Stockholm-
based My Little Drama in 2008 where
they showcase and sell their collaborative
jewellery. The two have known each other
since 1978 when they used to draw sad
puppies at kindergarten. The collection
consists of a number of motifs that all
have their own unique character. Some
are vain, some are cheeky, others live
their life on a string.

N

Nous Vous |
nousvous.eu

Nous Vous (We You) is a British visual
communications collective. They are
predominately a graphic design, art
direction and illustration studio, working
both as individuals and as a team on a
wide range of projects. They also initiate
art and design-based projects which
develop and explore their eponymous
collective spirit. Nous Vous show work
internationally and around the UK,
curate frequent exhibitions and have an
annual publication entitled *Pocket Sized*
which features work from a variety of
contributors. Nous Vous is: William
Edmonds, Jay Cover, Tom Hudson
and Nicolas Burrows.

P

Peepshow |
peepshow.org.uk
peepshop.org.uk

With its physical base in East London,
the ten-people strong Peepshow have
steadily built a reputation for producing
intelligent, unique, surprising, beautiful
and personal work. Much of the creative
input for their commercial output stems
from the extracurricular activities they
engage in through various self-initiated
exhibitions and events worldwide.
Peepshow is: Luke Best, Jenny Bowers,
Miles Donovan, Chrissie Macdonald,
Pete Mellor, Marie O'Connor, Andrew
Rae, Elliot Thoburn, Lucy Vigrass and
Spencer Wilson. Clients include: BBC,
Kesselskramer, Mother, Wieden &
Kennedy, *Dazed & Confused*, The British
Council, Channel 4, Coca Cola, MTV, Nike,
Orange, Sony, Toyota, The Victoria and
Albert Museum and *Vogue*.

Mike Perry |
midwestisbest.com
untitled-a-magazine.com

Mike Perry works in Brooklyn, New York,
making books, magazines, newspapers,
clothing, drawings, paintings, illustrations
and teaching whenever possible. His first
book *Hand Job* (2006) and his second
book *Over & Over* (2008) were both
published by Princeton Architectural Press
and there are more books in the pipeline.
He launched his favourite self-published
magazine *Untitled a...* in 2007. Clients
include *New York Times Magazine,
Dwell Magazine*, Microsoft Zune, Urban
Outfitters, eMusic and Zoo York.

peter&wendy |
peter-wendy.com
xavierencinas.com

Graphic designer Xavier Encinas and his
Paris-based design studio peter&wendy
produce a variety of graphic projects
in print, publishing, exhibition and
event identity, corporate identity and
anything else that gets them excited to
get involved.

Platform Skateboarding |
platformboards.co.uk
splendid-industrial.co.uk

UK-based Platform is the creative outlet
of designers Jeremy Owen and Chris
Carus who both also have separate day
jobs. One of them works in exhibition
design, the other in publishing.

Plushood |
plushood.com
go-tam.com

Plushood is the company of product
designer Shlomi Schillinger, a graduate
from Israel's Holon Institute of Technology
and Design, and Tamar Moshkovitz (also
known as TAM), an illustrator, designer
and animator who graduated from the
visual communication department at
Wizo Haifa College of Design. When not
working on their own solo projects the
pair produce and distribute *Plushoods* –
a series of plush dolls with five unique
characters. The *Plushoods* were launched
in 2006 and feature screen-printed
graphics. The dolls are all handmade
in Israel.

R

Revenge is Sweet |
revengeissweet.org

Angelique Piliere from France and Lee
Owens from Australia met while studying
design in Australia and now live and work
together in London where they set up
Revenge is Sweet in 2007. After working
in various London studios, Revenge is
Sweet now produce work under their
own name, crossing the lines between
illustration, design and typography.

Rinzen |
rinzen.com

Australian design and art collective Rinzen is best known for the collaborative approach of its five members. With their 2001 book, the group invited over 30 international participants to sequentially rework digital art, in what has now become a common method of collaboration among graphic designers and illustrators. Rinzen's work, created both individually and as a collective, embraces a wide range of styles and techniques, often featuring bold, geometric designs or intricate, hand-drawn studies. Rinzen's posters and album covers have been exhibited at the Louvre in Paris, and their large-scale artworks are installed in Tokyo's Zero Gate and Copenhagen's Hotel Fox. They designed the inaugural issue of Paul Pope's *Batman* for DC Comics and graphics for a bicycle released by Japanese company Bebike. Members of the group are currently based in Berlin, Brisbane, Melbourne and New York.

Alex Robbins |
alexrobbins.co.uk

Alex Robbins is a freelance illustrator and graphic designer who graduated from Camberwell College of Arts, London. He has an experimental approach to image-making, using a variety of tools and skills with each project he undertakes. His work has been published in numerous books and magazines and his clients include *The New York Times*, *The Guardian*, *The New Yorker*, *Time Out*, Dunlop Shoes, *Reader's Digest*, Rojo and Macleans.

Joe Rogers, Colourbox |
colourboxonline.com
colourboxshop.bigcartel.com

Joe Rogers runs illustration and graphic design practice and shop Colourbox, based near Birmingham, UK. Colourbox works in all areas of design and illustration, producing contemporary designs for both national and international editorial, advertising and corporate clients, including French cultural magazine *Standard*, American-based *Let Go* magazine and online arts magazine *Iniciativa Colectiva*. Colourbox also produced T-shirt designs for Japan-based retailer Graniph, illustrations on tote bags for French design company LoveBy, and branding for American musician Peter Hadar and 3Sided Photography.

S

Emmi Salonen |
emmi.co.uk

Originally from Finland, Emmi Salonen graduated from the University of Brighton in the UK in 2001 with a BA in graphic design. After moving to Italy to work at Fabrica, Benetton's controversial young designers' melting pot, she worked at karlssonwilker in New York, before starting her own practice, Emmi, in London in 2005. She divides her time between commissioned work, working as a sessional tutor at Ravensbourne and New Bucks Universities and self-initiated projects such as her popular button badges.

Birgit Simons |
birgitsimons.de

Frankfurt-based graphic designer Birgit Simons lived in Japan for over three years from 2005. The density of inspiration and the new exotic environment had a deep impact on her design. In 2007 she relaunched her sideline BBags – bags and accessories made of vintage materials – this time using Japanese *obi*, the beautiful and colourful sash that ties the kimono.

Sing Statistics |
singstatistics.co.uk
eveningtweed.com
abouttoday.co.uk

Edinburgh-based Sing Statistics are graphic designer Jez Burrows and illustrator Lizzy Stewart. Their first book *I Am The Friction* from 2008 is written by Burrows and illustrated by Stewart.

Andy Smith |
asmithillustration.com

Andy Smith graduated from the Royal College of Art in London in 1998. Since then he has worked as an illustrator for clients such as Nike, Expedia, Mercedes, Vauxhall and Orange. As well as commercial work, he produces self-published books and silkscreen prints.

Astrid Stavro |
astridstavro.com
artofthegrid.com

Italian-born Astrid Stavro runs her own design studio SAS (Studio Astrid Stavro) in Barcelona. In addition to running the studio, SAS also runs El Palace Editions, El Palace Exhibitions and El Palace Products, a small, self-initiated publishing company that explores ideas and their visual offsprings. Another self-initiated project by Stavro is the award-winning *Grid-it! notepads* that were initially developed and produced during her last two weeks at the Royal College of Art. The first *Art of the Grid* shelving units were also produced during that period.

Maja Sten |
majasten.se
mylittledrama.com

Stockholm-based freelancer Maja Sten studied at London's Royal College of Art where she graduated in Communication Art and Design in 2002. Besides her commissioned work and her involvement in My Little Drama she also creates self-initiated work.

Subcommunication |
subcommunication.com
subtitude.com

Canadian graphic designer Valérie Desrochers and Switzerland-born Sébastien Théraulaz run Montréal-based design studio Subcommunication. They divide their time between commissioned work and self-initiated projects, such as passionately designing fonts they release via their sideline department, Subtitude.

Supersentido |
supersentido.cl

Artist and designer Pablo 'Pece' Castro, aka Supersentido, is based in Santiago, Chile. He divides his time between his day job as art director for an advertising agency and his self-initiated work, which has been exhibited and published across Latin America and Europe. He designs garments and T-shirts, loves street art and art toys. He started his self-published project *La Nueva Galerìa de Bolsillo (LNGB)* – the new pocket gallery – in 2005, featuring his own work and that of other street artists.

Kate Sutton |
katesutton.co.uk
katesutton.etsy.com

Since graduating from university, where she studied graphic arts, Kate Sutton has been working as a freelance illustrator. As well as taking part in multiple exhibitions, Sutton has worked with clients such as Howies, Roxy, Urban Outfitters and Nookart. Ornate patterns and car boot sales rank among the main influences on her work. She creates many different products, ranging from badges to plush toys, that are all lovingly hand-crafted.

Swigg Studio |
thisisswigg.com

Stephanie Wenzel is a graphic artist living and working in Brooklyn, New York. In 2004 she founded Swigg Studio, a multi-disciplinary design firm, as well as *Swigg Products!*, which creates tactile goods for human enjoyment including *SwiggStars!*, *Swigg Critters* and *Fungi Sculptures*.

T

TADO |
tado.co.uk

Sheffield-based illustration partnership Mike Doney and Katie Tang of TADO enjoy working across a huge range of projects, from advertising, illustration and fashion through to designer toys and various art shows. Mike and Katie are represented internationally by Debut Art, and exclusively in France by Tiphaine Illustration.

Stuart Tolley, Transmission |
thisistransmission.com
showbelow.co.uk

Brighton-based graphic designer Stuart Tolley founded his design studio Transmission in 2008. In 2007 he launched 'Show Below', an annual contemporary art exhibition, together with a few illustrators. Work is sold through the exhibition in Brighton and online.

Iro Tsavala |
iroillustration.gr

Recent Royal College of Art graduate Iro Tsavala is originally from Greece and based in London. She divides her time between commissioned projects and developing self-initiated projects dealing with narrative and small objects such as character dolls and screen-printed T-shirts. As an illustrator she is usually commissioned to make children's books, covers or other editorial work. She frequently self-publishes her own books.

Twopoints.Net |
twopoints.net
theoneweekendbookseries.com

Martin Lorenz, founder of Twopoints.Net, has received several prizes and is frequently featured in international books and magazines. Born in Hanover, Germany, Lorenz moved to Darmstadt at the age of 18 to study Communication Design. Three years later he moved to the Netherlands, learned Dutch, and graduated from the Royal Academy of Arts in The Hague. Martin and his wife Lupi live and work in Barcelona, where they have founded a corporation specializing in strategic design and communication. They teach in design schools, lecture and also organize design workshops. Self-initiated projects since 2000 include *The One Weekend Book Series*, *Chinese Whisper*, *Poster Series*, *Color Combinations* and *Cover Of The Week*.

V

Vier5 |
vier5.de
fairytale-magazine.com
vier5.de/fashiondepartment
v5-warehouse.com

Marco Fiedler and Achim Reichert both graduated in 1998 at Hochschule für Gestaltung, Offenbach, Germany. They set up their Paris-based design studio Vier5 in 2002 and one year later launched their bi-annual magazine, *Fairy Tale,* which reflects on fashion, photography, graphic design and art. Vier5 fashion department and their own fashion brand V5FD followed in 2007. The team also designs custom typefaces that are applied to self-initiated and commissioned projects.

Studio for Virtual Typography |
virtualtypography.com

Matthias Hillner was born in Germany, where he trained first in photography, then in visual design. He received his Masters degree in Communication Art and Design at the Royal College of Art in 2001, and has subsequently worked for various London-based design agencies. Matthias returned to the RCA in 2004 to study for an MPhil. His investigation into transitional typography led to the formation of the Studio for Virtual Typography, a design consultancy that specializes in developing typographic solutions for multimedia environments. The business development was supported by the NFTS (National Film and Television School), and sponsored by NESTA (National Endowment for Science, Technology and the Arts). Having worked as a sessional lecturer at Ravensbourne College of Design and Communication in Kent, and at the London Metropolitan University, Matthias was appointed course leader of Applied Graphics at Amersham and Wycombe University in Buckinghamshire in 2006. He also teaches typography at the University of Hertfordshire.

W

**Hanna Werning,
Spring Street Studio|**
byhanna.com

Hanna Werning works as an independent designer across various disciplines including communication and product design. She started working on her popular wallpaper-posters in 2001 and set up Spring Street Studio in Stockholm, Sweden, in 2004.

James West, Create/Reject |
createreject.com

Create/Reject was set up in 2006 by James West after he graduated from the London College of Communication. Most of his work is concept-driven for art, fashion and culture clients and is continually supported by a stream of self-initiated work including *Fifty Designers' Current Favourite Typefaces* – a book that raised £6,000 for UNICEF.

Simon Wild |
simonwild.com
simonwild.bigcartel.com

Cambridge School of Art graduate Simon Wild is a freelance illustrator. Inspired by travel and the collection of old toys that are kept in his studio, Wild creates illustrations that hint at a larger untold story. Simon has had his work featured in magazines, on music posters, album covers and projected on giant screens. He lives and works in Suffolk, England.

The Wizard's Hat |
thewizardshat.co.uk
mrbowlegs.co.uk
komadesign.co.uk

The Wizard's Hat is the outlet for collaborative collective Jeffrey Bowman and Andrew J. Miller. They have worked together since 2006, producing work and products that celebrate their love of illustration, design and art, and the obsessive habit of doodling. Their launch issue of *The Wizard's Hat* was released in 2008.

Z

Erin Zamrzla |
erinzam.com
erinzam.etsy.com

Designer, bookbinder and artist Erin Zamrzla is based in Santa Monica, California, where she runs her own design studio, freelances and takes on commissioned work. The majority of her projects are sold via the Internet.

Zeptonn |
zeptonn.nl

Born in Arnheim, the Netherlands, in 1979, designer Jan Willem Wennekes is also known by his alias, Stinger. Working as a freelance illustrator and graphic designer from his studio Zeptonn, in Groningen, he creates T-shirts, posters, logos, button badges, skateboards and books including *Stingermania* (2006) and *Black & White – Freedrawings* (2008). Stinger's trademark artistic style fuses imaginative objects with analytical twists. Jan has worked with a number of organizations, including Threadless, Blik, Popcling, TeeTonic, SplitTheAtom, Cut it Out and Playstation.

Zeroten |
zeroten.net

Zeroten is a London-based freelance artist and illustrator. *Exoskeletor* (2007) is his third and favourite zine so far. He graduated in graphic design in 2008 and now has a BA.

FL@33 |

flat33.com
stereohype.com
bzzzpeek.com
postcard-book.info

FL@33 is a multi-disciplinary studio for visual communication based in London. Its founders, Agathe Jacquillat (French, from Paris) and Tomi Vollauschek (Austrian, but from Frankfurt, Germany), studied at FH Darmstadt (Germany), Academy Julian/ESAG (Penninghen) (Paris), HDK (Gothenburg) and Camberwell College of Art (London), before they met on the Royal College of Art's postgraduate Communication Art and Design course in 1999.

They set up their company in London in 2001. The studio's clients include MTV Networks, BBC, Royal Festival Hall, Laurence King Publishing, *Creative Review, Computer Arts*, Groupe Galeries Lafayette, Matelsom, Arts Affaires and Friends of the Earth.

In 2004 they launched stereohype.com, Graphic Art & Fashion Boutique, as an international platform for both emerging and established talents. They have also released self-initiated projects such as the award-winning *Trans-form* magazine and online sound collection project bzzzpeek.com.

FL@33 interviews, features and company profiles have been published online, in numerous magazines, newspapers and books around the world. Interviews featured on BBC Radio and NPR, America's National Public Radio, after *The New York Times*, along with its international supplements, featured an article about the bzzzpeek.com project.

A FL@33 monograph was published in 2005 as part of the bilingual (English and French) design&designer book series by French Pyramyd Editions.

In 2008 Laurence King published *Postcard* – a book conceived, compiled, written, edited and designed by FL@33. Agathe and Tomi have also designed several other books, including Laurence King's *200%* and *300% Cotton New T-Shirt Graphics*, and *Patterns – New Surface Design*.

If you would like to submit your own self-initiated, self-published and commercially available project for potential inclusion in future editions of this book, please visit our dedicated website at madeandsold.com.

Photography credits

Nathan Beddows:
pages 59, 101, 171, 200–203
Sven Ellingen:
page 84
Stephen Lenthall:
pages 86–87, 182–183, 197
Anja Schaffner:
pages 108–109
Sølve Sundsbø:
page 111 (TypeFace)
Tonatiuh Ambrosetti:
pages 140–141
Arnaud Boulay:
pages 142–143
Steeve Beckouet:
page 181

Acknowledgements |

We would like to thank all of the people who responded to the call for entries for this book. We are very grateful for the number and quality of submissions we received, which exceed the number of pages available to us.

Special thanks must go to our publisher Laurence King and his team, especially Helen Evans, Susie May, Felicity Awdry and Angus Hyland.

We would also like to thank all of the contributors who made their valuable time available to us, to point us in the direction of other people's work, created or revised artworks especially for the book or prepared photoshoots for us.

Sincere thanks also go to these particularly inspiring and helpful people: Anne Brassier, Jon Burgerman, Mike Doney and Katie Tang, Anthony Burrill, Diego Vaisberg, Andrew Byrom, Kate Sutton, Lunartik JOnes, Tamar Moshkovitz, Miles Donovan, Alexander Egger, Alex Bec and Will Hudson, Jeremyville, Matt Burvill, Matthias Hillner, Sue Doeksen, Todd St. John, Peter Crnokrak, Achim Reichert and Marco Fiedler, Rilla Alexander, Mike Perry, Eivind Søreng Molvær, Judith Egger and Martin Lorenz.

And last but not least we would like to thank our clients, collaborators and supporters, and especially our families and friends.